TRACK LAYOUT DIAGRAMS
OF THE

LONDON & NORTHWESTERN
RAILWAY

R. D. FOSTER AND M. R. L. INSTONE

SECTION 5
NORTHAMPTONSHIRE

WSP

WILD SWAN PUBLICATIONS LTD.

© R. D. Foster and M. R. L. Instone 1988
ISBN 0 906867 62 2

Designed by Richard Foster
Typesetting by Berkshire Publishing Services
Printed by Amadeus Press, Huddersfield

Published by
WILD SWAN PUBLICATIONS LIMITED
1-3 Hagbourne Road, Didcot, Oxon OX11 8DP

CONTENTS

SECTION 5
NORTHAMPTONSHIRE

To Doncaster
Doncaster Engine Shed
NEWARK

Cotham

To Nottingham
Netherfield and Colwick Engine Shed
Nottingham Manvers Street Goods Yard

Saxondale Jc

Bottesford Junctions
North
West
East
South
To Grantham

GNR

BINGHAM ROAD

BARNSTONE

REDMILE

Section of line Melton Mowbray
to Bottesford and Saxondale
not included in this book.

Stathern Jc

HARBY & STATHERN

GNR

SCALFORD

MR MR

Sysonby Jc.

MELTON MOWBRAY

MR

MR

GREAT DALBY

JOHN O' GAUNT

Humberstone

GNR

Ingarsby

Marefield Jc. North
Marefield Jc. South

Thurnby &
Scraptoft

Lowesby

Marefield West Jc.

TILTON

LEICESTER

MR

EAST NORTON
East Norton Tunnel

HALLATON

Pain's Siding

Thorpe-by-Water LC

Liddington LC

MEDBOURNE

Great Easton LC

ROCKINGHAM

UPPINGHAM

Uppingham Junction

MORCOTT

LUFFENHAM (not included in this book)
South Luffenham LC
Luffenham LC

WAKERLEY & BARROWDEN

Monckton's Siding

GNR (S & ER)
From Stamford

To Grantham

Bell's Siding

SEATON

KINGSCLIFFE

Yarwell Jc
Wansford Tunnel

WANSFORD

CASTOR

GNR

ORTON WATERVILLE

Fletton Road Jc GER

To March

Fletton Jc

Longville Jc
Woodstone Wharf

PETER-
BOROUGH

GNR
From
London

Naylor Benzon's Sdg

NASSINGTON

ELTON

OUNDLE

Elmington LC

Gypsy Lane LC
Oundle Ballast Pit

BARNWELL
Barnwell L.C.
Wigsthorpe L.C.

THRAPSTON

THORPE

1 Langton
2 Welham Sidings
3 Welham Junction
4 Weston L.C.
5 ASHLEY & WESTON
6 Holt's Siding
7 Holt L.C.
8 Drayton Junction
9 Drayton L.C.

A Duston North Junction
B NORTHAMPTON BRIDGE STREET
C Hardingstone Junction
D Bedford Road Crossing
E Little Houghton Siding
F Cogenhoe L.C.
G Cogenhoe Siding
H Whiston Siding

3
4 5 6 7 8 9
1
2

Great Bowden Jc (site of)

MARKET HARBOROUGH

LUBENHAM
Scoboro' LC

THEDDINGWORTH
Husband's Bosworth LC

WELFORD & KILWORTH

South Kilworth LC

LILBOURNE

YELVERTOFT &
STANFORD PARK

CLIFTON MILL

RUGBY

KILSBY & CRICK
Crick Tunnel
Watford Tunnel

Watford Lodge

LONG BUCKBY

CHURCH BRAMPTON

Dallington Heath

NORTHAMPTON CASTLE

Duston West Jc

Duston Siding

Rothersthorpe Crossing

BLISWORTH

ROADE

SMJ

From Euston SECTION 3

Little Bowden Xing
Oxendon Tunnels

CLIPSTON & OXENDON

KELMARSH
Kelmarsh Tunnels
Green Lane LC
Draughton Siding

LAMPORT
Hanging Houghton LC

Lamport Ironstone Sidings

BRIXWORTH

SPRATTON

Attenboro' & Co's Sidings
Merry Tom LC

PITSFORD & BRAMPTON

Pitsford Ironstone Siding

Boughton Crossing

Kingsthorpe Jc

ALTHORP PARK

MR

MR

Newbridge Sidings

Islip Iron Ore Co's Sdgs
Woodford Mill LC
Woodford Sidings (later Keeble's Sdg)

RINGSTEAD

Butlin's Siding

IRTHLINGBOROUGH (HIGHAM FERRERS)
Irthlingboro' Iron Ore Co's Sidings
Rixon & Whitehouse's Siding

DITCHFORD

MR

WELLINGBOROUGH

Doddington L.C.

Hardwater Crossing

A D E
F G H

BILLING

CASTLE ASHBY

Hunsbury Hill Tunnel

Middleton

B C

LNWR lines included in this book

LNWR & GNR Joint lines included
in this book

LNWR & GNR Joint lines not
included in this book

Other LNWR lines

Other Railways

TRACK LAYOUT DIAGRAMS OF THE L.N.W.R.
SECTION 5 – NORTHAMPTONSHIRE

This volume sets out to cover the majority of lines which formed the Northampton, Nottingham and Peterborough District of the L.N.W.R. It includes the portion of main line between Roade and Rugby via Northampton (the Northampton Loop or New Line) but not the original main line via Blisworth which will appear in Section 3.

With the exception of the Northampton Loop, the lines covered by this volume are largely the rural secondary routes and branches which radiated north and eastwards from Northampton, Blisworth and Rugby towards Market Harborough, Peterborough, Stamford and Nottingham. The routes and layouts were the subject of extensive development and enlargement during the late 1870s and early 1880s and indeed the majority of the lines were opened or doubled during this period. The most important of these events was the opening in 1879 of the G.N. and L.N.W. joint line through Melton Mowbray which opened up the Nottinghamshire Coalfield to exploitation by the L.N.W.R., and the opening in 1880-2 of the Northampton Loop line. The latter effectively provided the last link in a chain intended to give the L.N.W.R. four lines of way continuously from Euston to Rugby. Of the lines covered in the book, the Northampton Loop is now the only one still open to passengers. The majority of the secondary routes and branches were closed during the 1960s as a result of the 1963 report, 'Reshaping of British Railways' (more commonly known as the Beeching Plan).

The section of the G.N. and L.N.W. joint line between Welham Junction and Melton Mowbray was maintained by the L.N.W.R. and has been included in the book. The section north of Melton was maintained by the G.N.R. and is therefore not included. The joint line was important principally as a freight line conveying coal south from the Nottinghamshire Coalfield to London. Something of the importance of this traffic can be judged from the fact that the L.N.W.R. maintained an eight-road engine shed at Colwick.

The Northamptonshire area was rich in ironstone deposits and these were extensively exploited to feed the iron-making industry. The sidings and facilities provided for the ironstone miners and quarries were a notable feature of many of the lines depicted in this book. Further information on the mines and their railways can be obtained from *The Ironstone Railways of the Midlands* by E. S. Tonks (1959), currently being revised and issued in parts.

In compiling this volume the authors gratefully acknowledge the assistance of the following: Northamptonshire Record Office, Northampton Public Library, Wellingborough Public Library, Cambridgeshire Record Offices, Peterborough Divisional Library, Leicestershire Record Office, Leicester Public Library, Leicester University Library, Birmingham Central Reference Library, Public Record Office, Kew, National Library of Scotland, National Railway Museum, M. Christensen and G.M. Webb.

Our thanks are due to M. Christensen and A. O. McDougall for checking the drafts, and to Barbara Davis, June Judge and Paul Karau for their assistance in producing this book.

LOCATION AND LINE NUMBERING

The location numbering used in this book is part of a system devised by the Signalling Record Society which will eventually cover all main line railways in the United Kingdom.

Two letters and six figures uniquely identify any station, signal cabin, ground frame, level crossing, etc. The letters identify the pre-1922 company (NW for London and North Western Railway in this case) and the first three figures are a line number. The main lines are given 'king' numbers (001, 010, 020, 030, etc.). These are followed by the branches off the 'king' line, generally in the order in which they diverge from it working in the down direction. Each main line has an individual number except for a few of the longer routes such as the West Coast Main Line which is split into more manageable geographical parts. The West Coast line, for example, is divided at Watford, Rugby, Stafford, Crewe, and so on, producing lines 001, 030, 070, 085, etc.

On each line, signal cabins, ground frames and other locations are listed along the line in order, running in the down direction. Stations and tunnels are given separate numbers only where the system would not otherwise identify them.

To assist readers, indexes including the location numbers, are given both alphabetically and in line order. Examination of these and the diagrams should enable the numbering system to be understood.

ABBREVIATIONS

GENERAL

A.H.B.s	Automatic Half Barriers
A.O.C.L.	Automatic Open Crossing locally monitored
A.O.C.R.	Automatic Open Crossing remotely monitored
B.E.A.	British Electricity Authority
Br.	Bridge
c	circa
C.C.E.	Chief Civil Engineer
C.E.A.	Central Electricity Authority
C.E.G.B.	Central Electricity Generating Board
C.M. & E.E.	Chief Mechanical and Electrical Engineer
Co.	Company
C.P.s	Cattle Pens
C.S.	Coal Stage
D.C.E.	Divisional Civil Engineer
D.G.L.	Down Goods Loop
D.H.L.B.s	Double Half Lifting Barriers
D.R.S.	Down Refuge Siding
E.S.	Engine Shed
Ft	Feet
F.L.B.s	Full Lifting Barriers
G.F.	Ground Frame
G.S.	Goods Shed
H.	Halt
H.L.	High Level
I.B.S.	Intermediate Block Signals
i.c.w.	in connection with
Jc	Junction
L.C.	Level Crossing
L.D.	Loading Dock
L.L.	Low Level
M.A.S.	Multiple Aspect Signalling
M.H.B.	Manned Half Barriers
M.o.D.	Ministry of Defence
M.o.F.	Ministry of Food
M.o.W.	Ministry of Works
M.P.	Mile Post
N.C.L.	National Carriers Ltd.
O.E.S.D.	Ordnance and Explosives Supply Depot
P.S.A.	Private Siding Agreement
P.S.A.T.	Private Siding Agreement Terminated
R.C.E.	Regional Civil Engineer
R.S.	Refuge Siding
S & T	Signal and Telegraph
S.C.	Signal Cabin
Sdg.	Siding
S.L.W.	Single Line Working
t.o.u.	Taken out of use
T.T.	Turntable
U.G.L.	Up Goods Loop
U.R.S.	Up Refuge Siding
w.e.f.	With effect from
W.M.	Weighing Machine
Xing	Crossing
yds	Yards

RAILWAY COMPANIES

B.R.	British Railways
G.E.R.	Great Eastern Railway
G.N.R.	Great Northern Railway
L.M.S.R.	London Midland and Scottish Railway
L.N.W.R.	London and North Western Railway
M.R.	Midland Railway
S. & E.R.	Stamford and Essindine Railway
S.M.J.	Stratford on Avon and Midland Junction
G.C.R.	Great Central Railway

SYMBOLS

⧖	Signal Cabin
■	Ground Frame
⋈	Gate
▽	Mile Post

LINE NW050 ROADE TO RUGBY — New Line or Northampton Loop
Line opened Roade to Northampton (Castle) to Goods 1.8.1881
Line opened Roade to Northampton (Castle) to Passengers 3.4.1882

MIDDLETON

1906

HUNSBURY HILL TUNNEL
115 yards

64.1   64.57

NW050.021

To Sand Pit (used
as tip from c.1923)

62½ ▽

Third siding added bw 1910

Middleton Frame
Brought into use 13/15.2.1965
t.o.u.   11.6.1967

NW050.013

DOWN MAIN →
← UP MAIN

From
Roade
See Line NW030
(Section 3)

Br. 11 (later 6)   Br. 12 (later 7)

Middleton S.C. 62.45
Opened   1.8.1881
Closed 13/15.2.1965 (M.A.S.)

NW050.012

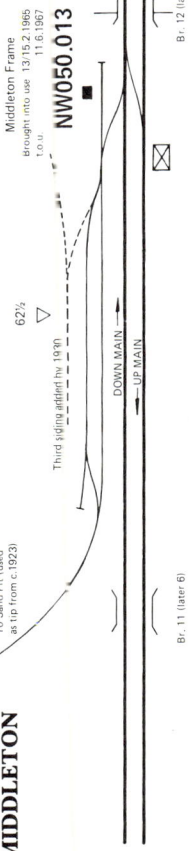

S.C. Originally block cabin only
Crossover brought into use (15) 1.9.1890
Sidings and connections brought into use (22) 10.1906
Sidings t.o.u. 8.6.1965. Crossover t.o.u. 11.6.1967

DUSTON JUNCTION WEST

See also pages 10 & 11

1882

Br. 24 (later 19)

Br. 23 (later 18)

DOWN MAIN →
← UP MAIN

DOWN
UP

Private Line

Duston Junction West S.C. 65.09
Opened 6.1881
High level frame brought into use 1.8.1881
Signal Cabin ceased to be a block post
on the H.L. Line 13/15.2.1965 (M.A.S.)
Closed 10.1969

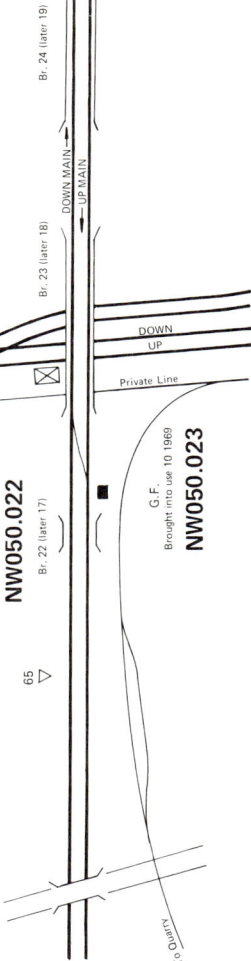

NW050.022

65 ▽

Br. 22 (later 17)

G.F.
Brought into use 10.1969

NW050.023

To Quarry

NORTHAMPTON CASTLE

1875

Line from Duston Junction to Market Harborough opened 16.2.1859.
This portion later became part of the Northampton Loop which
joined it at the south end of Northampton Castle and left it at
Kingsthorpe.

To Market
Harborough
Line NW054
(Page 21)

RIVER   VIADUCT 0.68

NENE

0.64

← UP MAIN

NORTHAMPTON CASTLE STATION

DOWN MAIN

VIADUCT
0.55

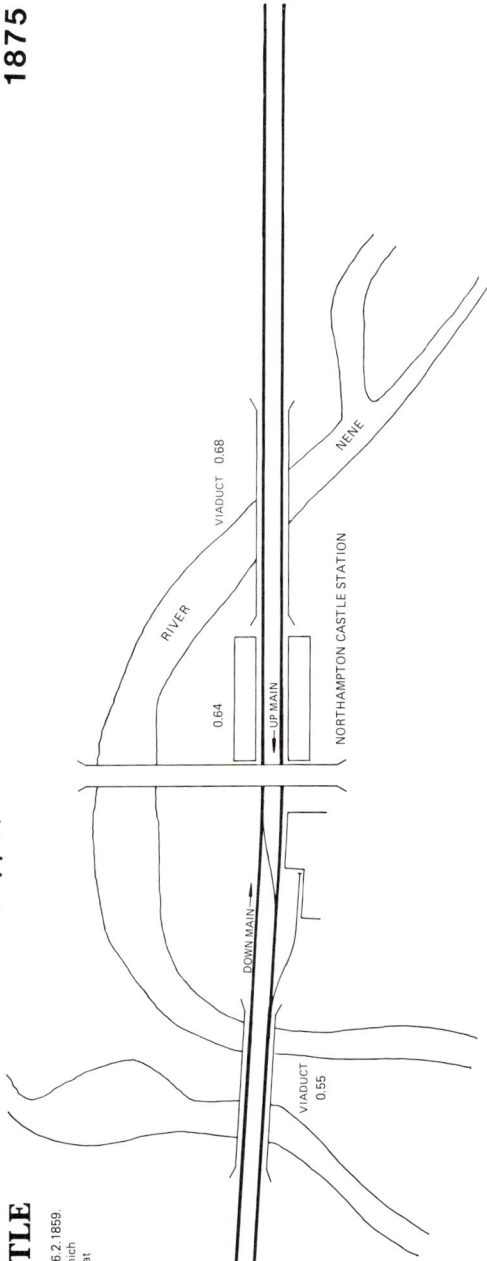

From Blisworth
(Duston Junction)
Lines NW051 & NW052
(Pages 9 & 10)

LINE NW050

NORTHAMPTON CASTLE

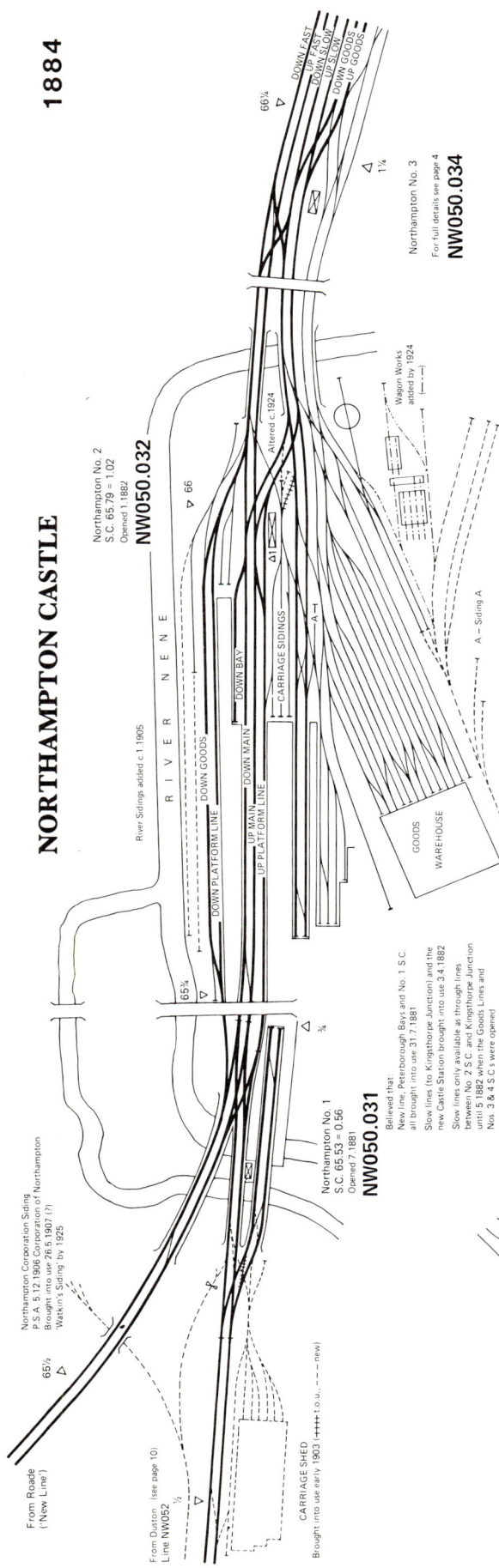

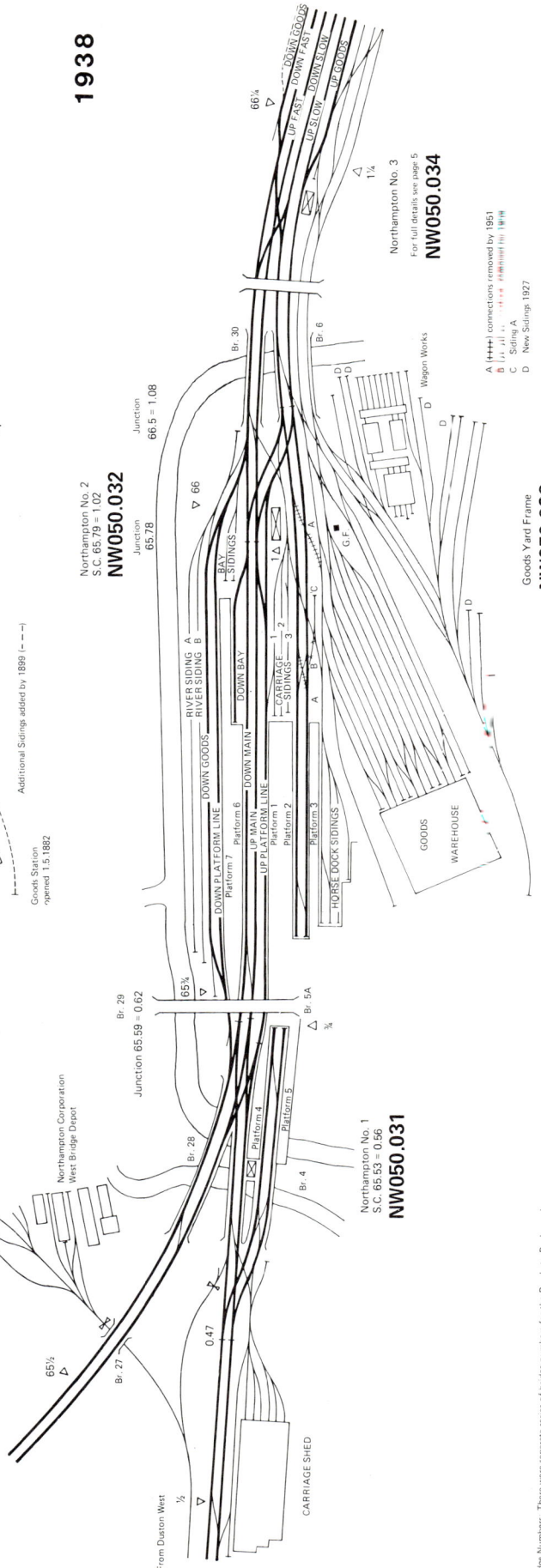

1884

From Roade
('New Line')

Northampton Corporation Siding
P.S.A. 5.12.1906 Corporation of Northampton
Brought into use 26.5.1907 (?)
Watkin's Siding by 1925

From Duston
Line NW052

Brought into use early 1903 (++++ t.o.u. _ . _ . — new)

CARRIAGE SHED

65½ ▽

¾ ▽

Northampton No. 1
S.C. 65.53 = 0.56
Opened 7.7.1881

NW050.031

Believed that:
New line, Peterborough Bays and No 1 S.C.
all brought into use 31.7.1881
Slow lines (to Kingsthorpe Junction) and the
new Castle Station brought into use 3.4.1882
Slow lines only available as through lines
between No 2 S.C. and Kingsthorpe Junction
until 1.5.1882 when the Goods Lines and
Nos 3 & 4 S.C.1 were opened

RIVER NENE

River Sidings added c.1.1905

DOWN PLATFORM LINE
DOWN GOODS
DOWN MAIN
DOWN BAY
UP MAIN
UP PLATFORM LINE
CARRIAGE SIDINGS

Northampton No. 2
S.C. 65.79 = 1.02
Opened 1.1882

NW050.032

66 ▽

△ 1

Altered c.1924

Wagon Works
added by 1924

GOODS
WAREHOUSE

Goods Station
opened 1.5.1882

Additional Sidings added by 1899

A — Siding A

A

65¾ ▽

66¾ ▽

1¼ ▽

DOWN FAST
DOWN SLOW
UP SLOW
UP GOODS
DOWN GOODS

Northampton No. 3
For full details see page 4

NW050.034

1938

From Duston West

½ ▽

CARRIAGE SHED

Br. 27

0.47

Northampton Corporation
West Bridge Depot

Br. 28

Br. 29

Junction 65.59 = 0.62

65½ ▽

¾ ▽

Br. 4

Br. 5A

Platform 4

Platform 5

Northampton No. 1
S.C. 65.53 = 0.56

NW050.031

DOWN PLATFORM LINE
Platform 7
DOWN GOODS
DOWN MAIN
DOWN BAY
BAY SIDINGS
RIVER SIDING A
RIVER SIDING B
Platform 6
UP MAIN
UP PLATFORM LINE
Platform 1
Platform 2
Platform 3
CARRIAGE SIDINGS
HORSE DOCK SIDINGS
A
B
C

Northampton No. 2
S.C. 65.79 = 1.02

NW050.032

66 ▽

Junction
65.78

Junction
66.5 = 1.08

Br. 30

Br. 6

1 △

1
2
3

A
C

G.F.

GOODS
WAREHOUSE

Wagon Works

D
D
D
D
D

Goods Yard Frame

NW050.033

65¾ ▽

66¾ ▽

1¼ ▽

DOWN FAST
DOWN SLOW
UP FAST
UP SLOW
UP GOODS

Northampton No. 3
For full details see page 5

NW050.034

A (++++) connections removed by 1951
B ( ) connections removed by 1951
C Siding A
D New Sidings 1927

Bridge Numbers There were separate series of bridge numbers for the Roade to Rugby and
Duston to Market Harborough lines even to the extent of some bridges having two numbers.

NORTHAMPTON CASTLE

1961

NORTHAMPTON CASTLE STATION 65.68

Northampton No. 2 S.C. 65.79 = 1.02

NW050.032

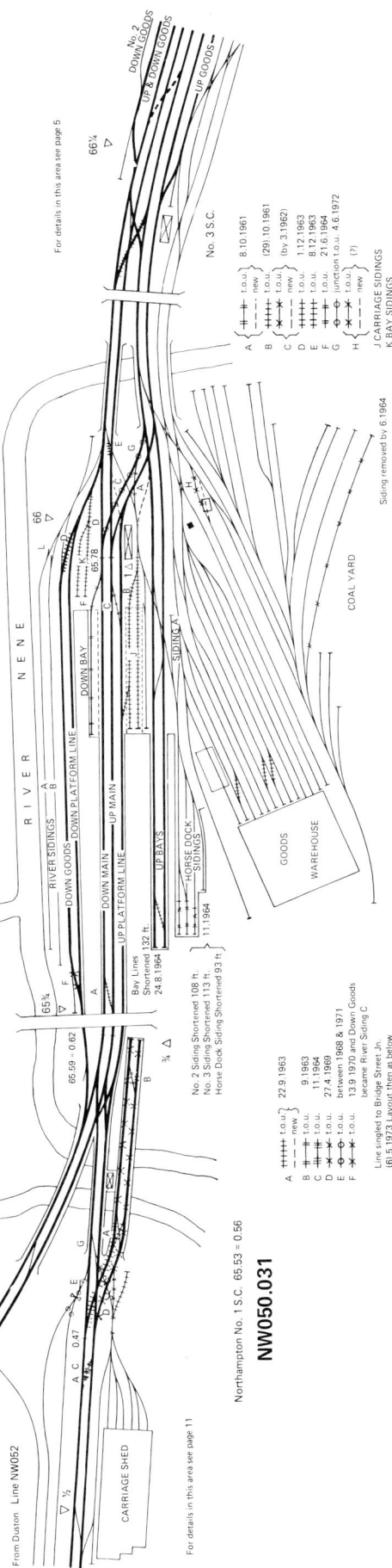

For details in this area see page 5

66¼ ▽

DOWN No. 2 GOODS
UP & DOWN GOODS
UP GOODS

No. 3 S.C.

RIVER NENE

A	⊢⊢⊢⊢ t.o.u.	8.10.1961
	− − − − new	(29).10.1961
B	⊢⊩⊩⊩ t.o.u.	(by 3.1962)
C	⊢⊩⊱⊱ t.o.u.	1.12.1963
D	⊢⊱⊱⊱ new	8.12.1963
E	⊢⊱⊱⊱ t.o.u.	21.6.1964
F	⊢⊶⊶⊶ junction t.o.u.	4.6.1972
G	⊶⊶⊶
H	⊶⊱⊱ t.o.u.	(?)
	⊱⊱ new

J CARRIAGE SIDINGS
K BAY SIDINGS
L Trap points in River Sidings A & B removed 13.9.1970

66 ▽

Siding removed by 6.1964

COAL YARD

RIVER SIDINGS A
B
DOWN GOODS
DOWN PLATFORM LINE
DOWN MAIN
UP PLATFORM LINE
DOWN BAY
UP BAYS
SIDING A
HORSE DOCK SIDINGS

65.78
L
K
F
C
B
A
H

Bay Lines Shortened 132 ft. 24.8.1964

11.1.1964

GOODS WAREHOUSE

No. 2 Siding Shortened 108 ft.
No. 3 Siding Shortened 113 ft.
Horse Dock Siding Shortened 93 ft.

A	⊢⊢⊢⊢ t.o.u.	22.9.1963
B	⊢⊩⊩⊩ new	9.1963
C	⊢⊩⊱⊱ t.o.u.	11.1964
D	⊢⊱⊱⊱ t.o.u.	27.4.1969
E	⊢⊶⊱⊱ t.o.u.	between 1968 & 1971
F	⊢⊶⊱⊱ t.o.u.	

13.9.1970 and Down Goods became River Siding C.

Line singled to Bridge Street Jn. (6).5.1973 Layout then as below

G Trailing crossover t.o.u. 30.4/4.5.1973

65¾ ▽
65.59 = 0.62
¾ △

Northampton No. 1 S.C. 65.53 = 0.56

NW050.031

65½ ▽
½ △
0.47
A C
G
E D

Oil Depot

CARRIAGE SHED

From Duston Line NW052

For details in this area see page 11

1980

66¼ ▽

Br. 26

NW050.032

Northampton No. 2 S.C. 65.79
Closed 3.12.1982 and ⊢⊩ t.o.u.

Br. 25

Engineers Sidings
Cement unloading siding

66 ▽

RIVER SIDINGS A
B
C
DOWN PLATFORM LINE
DOWN MAIN
UP MAIN
UP PLATFORM LINE
CARRIAGE SIDING

Taylors Siding

7
9
11
13
15
17
19

N.C.L. Shed Demolished 1986

⊢⊩ t.o.u 4.11.1985

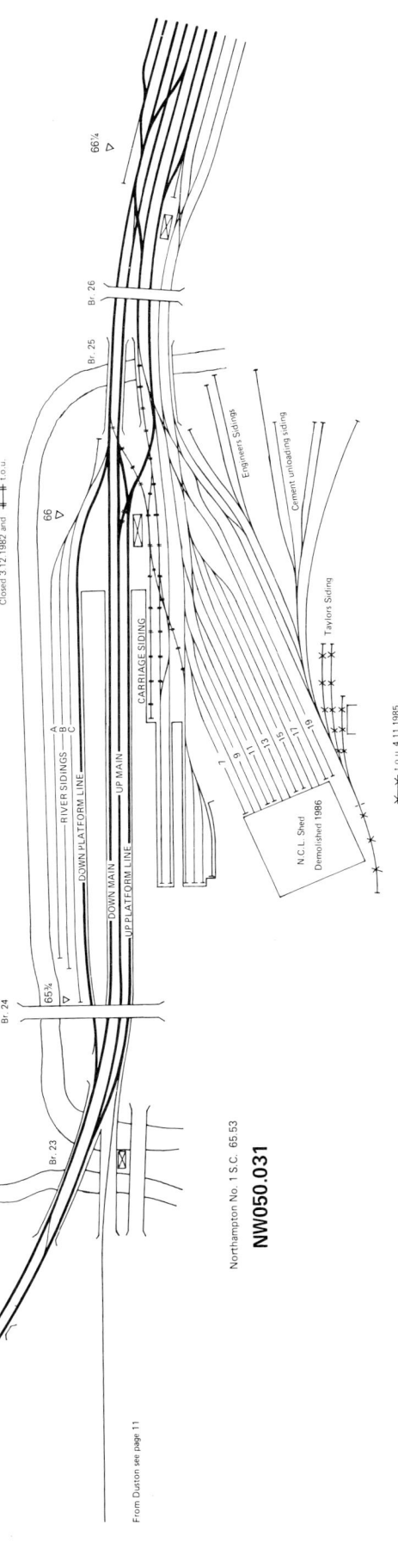

Goods Yard Frame
t.o.u 4.6.1972

NW050.033

Br. 24

65¾ ▽

Northampton No. 1 S.C. 65.53

NW050.031

Br. 23

Br. 22

65½ ▽

From Duston see page 11

NORTHAMPTON CASTLE YARDS

Apart from the connections at 1.15 this section was plain double line before 1882.
Slow lines Northampton to Kingsthorpe Junction opened for passenger trains 3.4 1882.
(Previously used for race traffic on 28.3 1882)
Nos. 3 & 4 Signal Cabins and Goods Lines opened about a month later.

1872

1884

1899

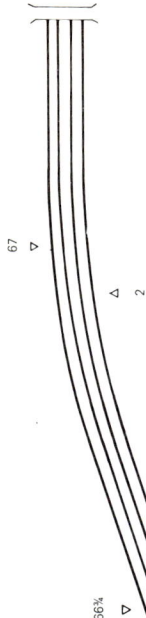

L.C.

1.15

66¾

1¼

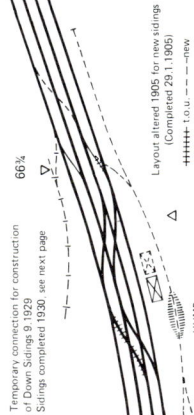

67

2

66¾

1¼

DOWN FAST
UP FAST
DOWN SLOW
UP SLOW
DOWN GOODS
UP GOODS

GOODS YARD LINES

Northampton No. 3 S.C.
66.16 = 1.19
Opened 2.5.1882
NW050.034

Northampton No. 4 S.C.
66.42 = 1.45
Opened c.5.1882
Closed c.6.1885
NW050.041

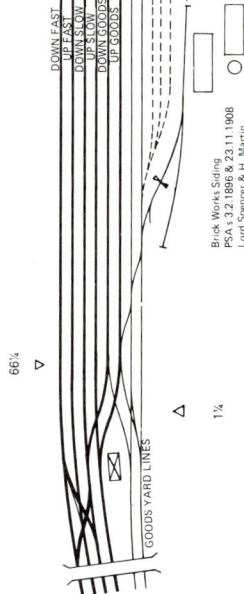

67

2

Temporary connection for construction
of Down Sidings 9.1929
Sidings completed 1930 see next page

Layout altered 1905 for new sidings
(Completed 29.1.1905)
+++++ I.O.U. ---- =new

66¾

1¼

HUMP

Northampton No. 4 S.C. 66.56 = 1.60
Opened c.1905?
Replaced by new cabin 1929
NW050.042
NW050.043

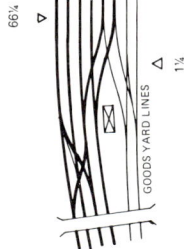

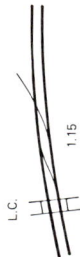

GOODS YARD LINES

Brick Works Siding
PSA's 3.2.1896 & 23.11.1908
Lord Spencer & H. Martin

66¾

1¼

Siding extended by 1928

Northampton No. 3 S.C. 66.16 = 1.19
NW050.034

NORTHAMPTON CASTLE YARDS

1938

Down Sidings G.F.
66.53
NW050.044

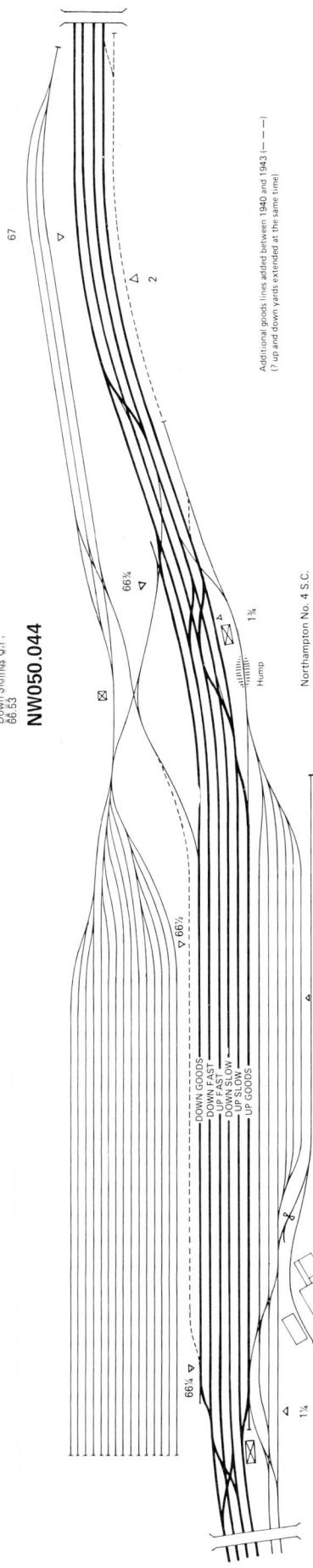

67

66½

2

Northampton No. 4 S.C.
66.56 = 1.60
NW050.043

DOWN GOODS
DOWN FAST
UP FAST
DOWN SLOW
UP SLOW
UP GOODS

Hump

1¾

66½

Martin's Siding

Brick Works

Timber Yard

1½

1¼

66½

Northampton No. 3 S.C.
66.16 = 1.19
NW050.034

Additional goods lines added between 1940 and 1943
(? up and down yards extended at the same time) (— — — —)

Down Sidings 20, 21, 22, 23 t.o.u. 3.9.1973, reinstated 19.11.1973.

1959

Down Sidings G.F.
66.53
t.o.u. 23.11.1986

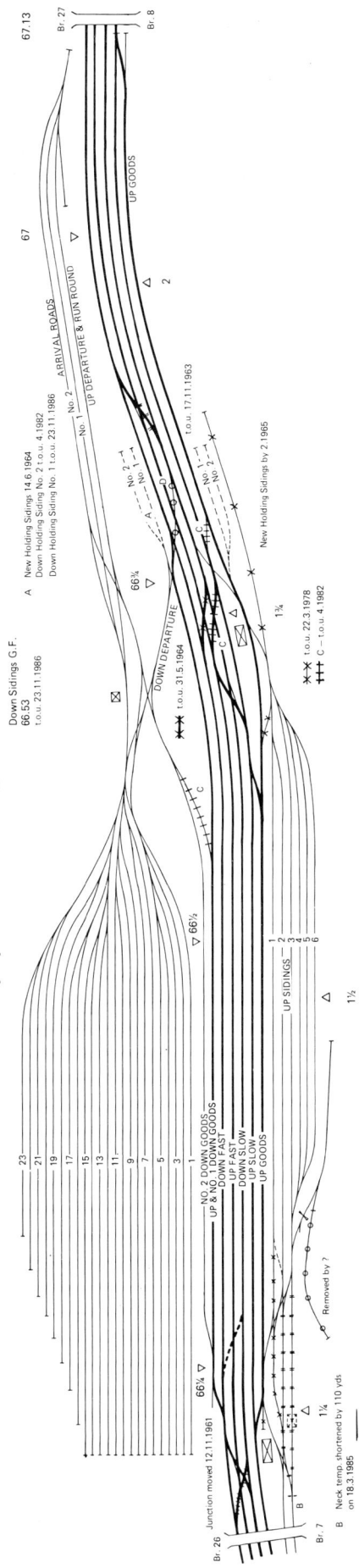

67.13
Br. 27
Br. 8

67

UP GOODS

2

ARRIVAL ROADS

UP DEPARTURE & RUN ROUND

No. 2
No. 1

A New Holding Sidings 14.6.1964
Down Holding Siding No. 2 t.o.u. 4.1982
Down Holding Siding No. 1 t.o.u. 23.11.1986

No. 2 t.o.u. 23.11.1986
No. 1 t.o.u. 17.11.1963

New Holding Sidings by 2.1965

66½

DOWN DEPARTURE

t.o.u. 31.5.1964

t.o.u. 22.3.1978

C - t.o.u. 4.1982

1¾

Northampton No. 4 S.C.
66.56 = 1.60
NW050.043

Down Sidings 1-23 t.o.u. Up Departure & Run Round and
Arrival Roads 1 & 2 renamed Engineers Sidings 1-3 respectively
and Holding Siding No. 1 and connection D t.o.u. 23.11.1986.

23
21
19
17
15
13
11
9
7
5
3
1

NO. 2 DOWN GOODS
UP & NO. 1 DOWN GOODS
DOWN FAST
DOWN SLOW
UP SLOW
UP GOODS

UP SIDINGS
1
2
3
4
5
6

66½

Removed by ?

Junction moved 12.11.1961

1¼

1½

Br. 26
Br. 7

Northampton No. 3 S.C.
66.16 = 1.19
Closed 1.11.1981
NW050.034

Northampton No. 3 S.C.
66.18
Opened 1.11.1981
NW050.035

B Neck temp. shortened by 110 yds on 18.3.1985
B Connections to Goods Yard Recovered 2.7.1978

Sidings altered 12.1963 (t.o.u.   — — — new)

No. 2 Down Goods renamed Up & No. 2 Down Goods
Up & No. 1 Down Goods renamed No. 1 Down Goods } 13/15.2.1965
Up Sidings 4, 5 & 6 t.o.u. 25.6.1978. Reinstated 2.7.1978

KINGSTHORPE JUNCTION

Line from Northampton to Kingsthorpe (approx) doubled Sept. 1861
Line from Kingthorpe to Lamport (NW054) doubled April 1862

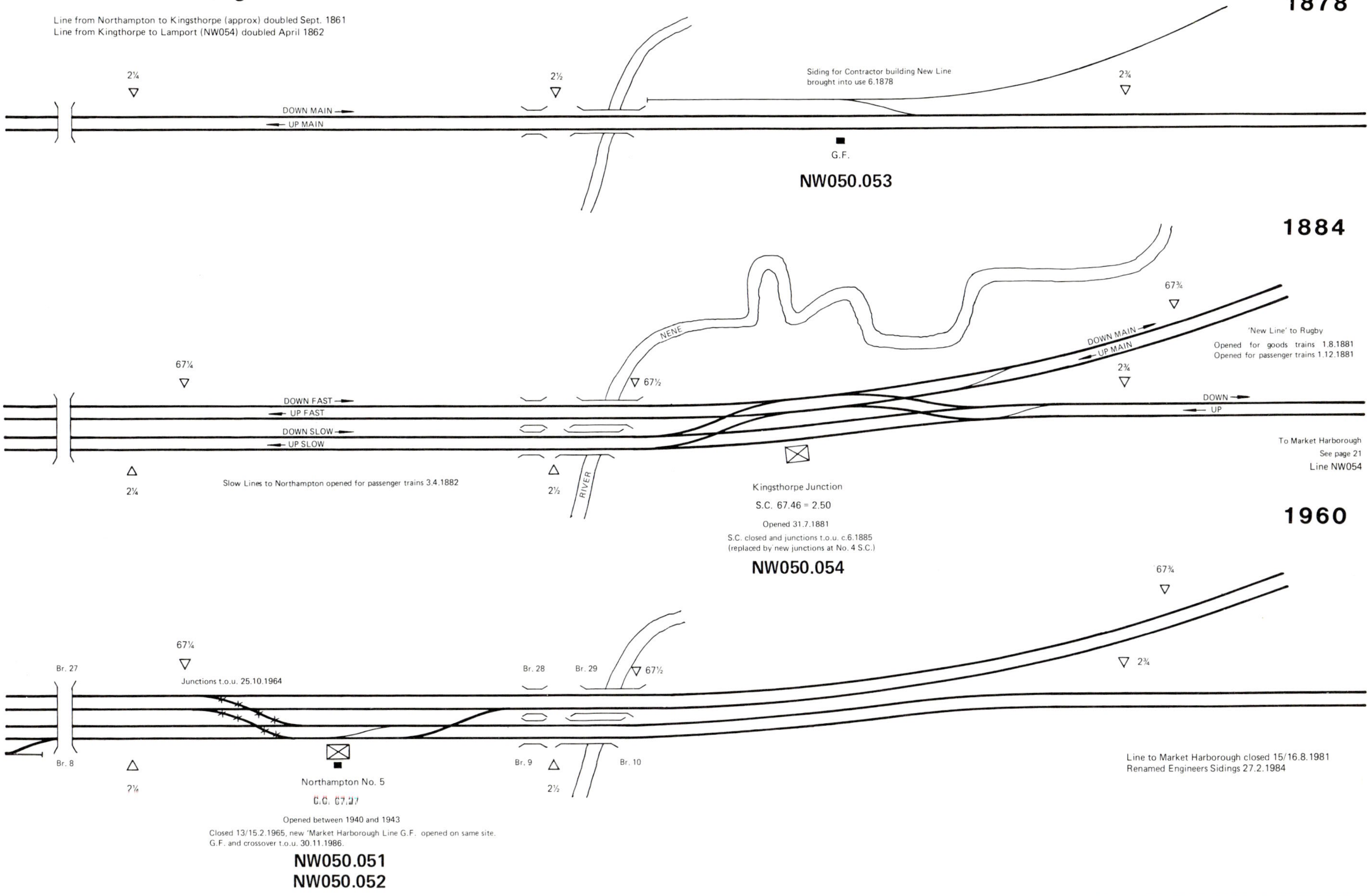

1878

DOWN MAIN
UP MAIN

2¼

Siding for Contractor building New Line
brought into use 6.1878

G.F.

NW050.053

1884

DOWN FAST
UP FAST
DOWN SLOW
UP SLOW

67¼

Slow Lines to Northampton opened for passenger trains 3.4.1882

NENE

67½

2¼

RIVER

'New Line' to Rugby
Opened for goods trains 1.8.1881
Opened for passenger trains 1.12.1881

DOWN
UP

67½

DOWN MAIN
UP MAIN

2¾

To Market Harborough
See page 21
Line NW054

Kingsthorpe Junction
S.C. 67.46 = 2.50
Opened 31.7.1881
S.C. closed and junctions t.o.u. c.6.1885
(replaced by new junctions at No. 4 S.C.)

NW050.054

1960

67¾

Junctions t.o.u. 25.10.1964

Northampton No. 5
G.G. 67.27

Opened between 1940 and 1943

Closed 13/15.2.1965, new 'Market Harborough' Line G.F. opened on same site.
G.F. and crossover t.o.u. 30.11.1986

**NW050.051
NW050.052**

Br. 27 Br. 8

Br. 28 Br. 9 Br. 29 Br. 10

67½ 2½

67¾

2½

Line to Market Harborough closed 15/16.8.1981
Renamed Engineers Sidings 27.2.1984

1918

CHURCH BRAMPTON

Br. 36

Levers

Levers

CHURCH BRAMPTON STATION
Opened 1.6.1912
Closed 18.5.1931

Platform levers removed 1918

NW050.063

69¾

DOWN MAIN
UP MAIN

Church Bampton S.C. 69.57 Approx
S.C. and crossover brought into use 9.1918
(Completed 21.7.1918)
S.C. closed c.1938 and replaced by I.B.S.
Crossover probably t.o.u. same date

NW050.062

1899

LINE NW050 ROADE TO RUGBY
Line Opened Kingsthorpe to Rugby to Goods 1.8.1881
Line Opened Kingsthorpe to Rugby to Passengers 1.12.1881

DALLINGTON HEATH

69

Br. 32

DOWN MAIN
UP MAIN

Crossover added 1898
(Completed 31.10.1898)

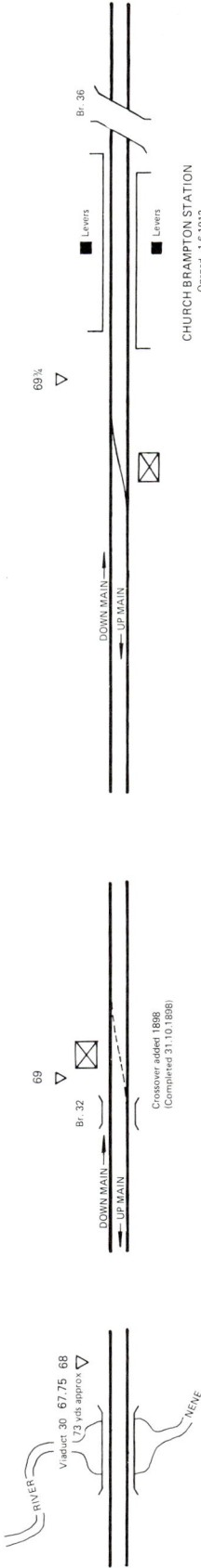

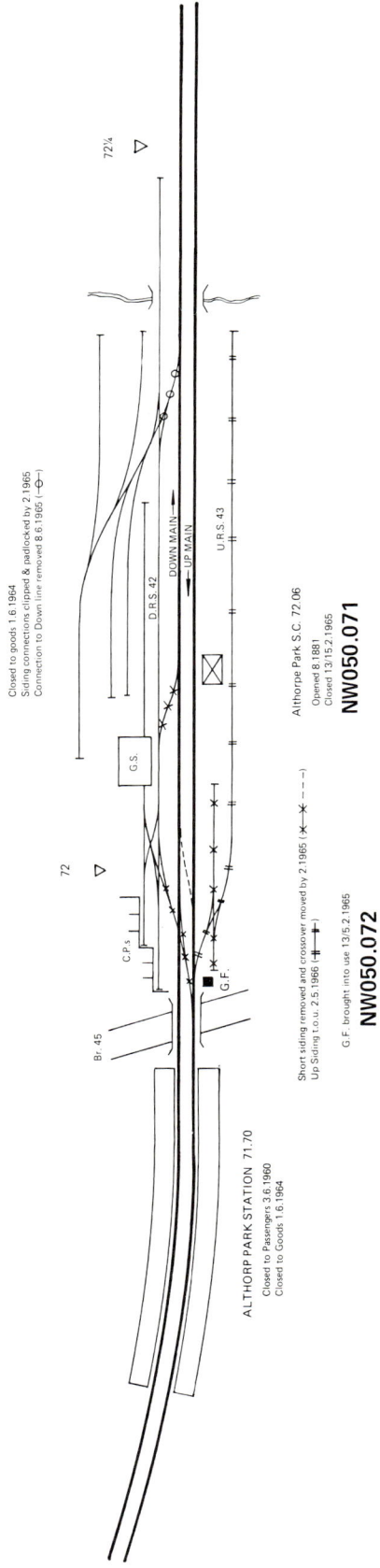

Dallington Heath S.C. 69.00
Opened 8.1881
Closed 1918 (?)

NW050.061

RIVER

Viaduct 30 67.75 68
(73 yds approx)

NENE

Up Main interlaced with Down Main over
Bridge 30 18.10.1981 to 24.1.1982

ALTHORP PARK

72¾

Closed to goods 1.6.1964
Siding connections clipped & padlocked by 2.1965
Connection to Down line removed 8.6.1965

DOWN MAIN
UP MAIN

D.R.S. 42

U.R.S. 43

G.S.

Althorpe Park S.C. 72.06
Opened 8.1881
Closed 13/15.2.1965

NW050.071

72

C.P.s

G.F.

Br. 45

ALTHORP PARK STATION 71.70

Closed to Passengers 3.6.1960
Closed to Goods 1.6.1964

Short siding removed and crossover moved by 2.1965
Up Siding t.o.u. 2.5.1966

G.F. brought into use 13/15.2.1965

NW050.072

LINE NW050

7

LONG BUCKBY

1899

Down Line Frame
Brought into use 13/15.2.1965
t.o.u. 1.6.1969

NW050.083

x—x t.o.u. (26).5.1962
Connections altered (26).5.1962 and —|—|— added
(— —|) new |—|—| t.o.u.

Up Line North Frame
Brought into use 13/15.2.1965
G.F. and crossover t.o.u. date not known

NW050.084

Long Buckby S.C. 75.55
Opened 8.1881
Closed 13/15.2.1965

NW050.081

Br: 59

75¾ ▽

D.R.S. 38

U.R.S. 54

G.S.

C.P.s

Closed to Goods 29.4.1968
Sidings t.o.u. 1.6.1969

x—x t.o.u. (19).5.1962

DOWN MAIN →
← UP MAIN

t.o.u. (29).10.1961

Horse Landing

Up Line South Frame
Brought into use 13/15.2.1965
t.o.u. 1.6.1969

NW050.082

Br: 58

Subway 57

75½ ▽

LONG BUCKBY STATION
75.38
Closed to Goods 29.4.1968

WATFORD LODGE

1899

78½ ▽

78¼ ▽

Br: 71

Br: 70

78.12

DOWN MAIN →
← UP MAIN

Up Loop brought into use late 1930

78.45

78.47

78.52

WATFORD TUNNEL
114 yds

Watford Lodge S.C. 78.43 Approx
Opened 1930
Closed 20.9.1964

NW050.092

78 ▽

Pulpit or Armchair Bridge
Br: 69

Watford Lodge S.C. 78.0
Opened 8.1881
Closed 1930

NW050.091

KILSBY & CRICK

1899

To Rugby
Line NW030
See Section 3

U.R.S. 42

Slip added by 9.1964

No. 2 Frame
Brought into use 20.9.1964

NW050.113

Kilsby & Crick S.C. 81.11
Opened 8.1881
Closed 20.9.1964

NW050.111

Connections t.o.u. by 9.1964

81 ▽

Br: 78

G.S.

C.P.s

x—x t.o.u. (16).12.1962

No. 1 Frame
Brought into use 20.9.1964

NW050.112

DOWN MAIN →
← UP MAIN

Closed to Goods 3.5.1965
Sidings & No. 1 Frame t.o.u. by 28.5.1965
(No. 2 Frame retained for signalling)

KILSBY & CRICK STATION
80.74
Closed to Passengers 1.2.1960
Closed to goods 3.5.1965

79½ ▽

CRICK TUNNEL
398 yds

NW050.101

Kilsby Ballast Pit: G.F. brought into use 8.1881 at this location.
Not known where it was situated or when removed

LINE N.W.051 BLISWORTH TO PETERBOROUGH
Section of line between BLISWORTH and NORTHAMPTON
Closed to passengers 4.1.1960. Closed completely 6.1.1969.
t.o.u. between Blisworth and Bridge St. Jc. 23.2.1969.

1884

DUSTON SIDINGS

ROTHERSTHORPE CROSSING

From Blisworth

Line NW030
See Section 3

Rothersthorpe S.C. 2.30

Closed 1.1969

NW051.011

To Quarries
Line to Quarries opened 1854/5

Duston Sidings S.C. 3.21
Canal Opened 1873

NW051.022

3¼ ▽

3½ △

All sidings on Up side new 18/3 for
Messrs. Lepper & Dodgson (completed 3.1873)

DOWN MAIN
UP MAIN

Ground Frame
Replaced 2.1881

NW051.021

G.F. 3.0

Iron Works

To Quarries
Duston Iron Ore Co.
G. E. Bevan & Co. Ltd. from 1863
Henry Higgins from 1880
Duston Iron Ore Co. Ltd. from 28.2.1885
Staveley Coal & Iron Co. @ 1909 (No P.S.A.)
Removed by 1923

To Quarries

1899

3½ △

3¼ ▽

S.C. 3.21
New S.C. opened 2.1898

NW051.023

Br. 7

W.M.

Connection & G.F. believed to have
been removed between 1905 & 1911

NW051.021

DOWN MAIN
UP MAIN

Hunsbury Hill Iron Works
Northampton Coal & Iron Co.
Ironworks erected 1873
Hunsbury Hill Coal & Iron Co. from 1875
Hunsbury Hill Iron Co. from 1888
P. Phipps
P. Phipps Executors
P.S.A. 26.3.1907 Executors of Pickering Phipps
Hunsbury Iron Co. from c.1922 (but works and mines closed 1921)
Richard Thomas & Co. from 1936 (only for dismantling of works)

3 ▽

Tramway from Quarries

1961

3½ △

Alterations to sidings by 1923 (✗ removed — new)
Further sidings removed by 1937 (╫ — ╫)

S.C. 3.21
Closed 13.9.1964

NW051.023

3¼ ▽

Down Siding t.o.u. (11).3.1962

Siding and crossover removed by 5.1964
Remaining sidings t.o.u. 13.9.1964

DOWN MAIN
UP MAIN

3 ▽

2.65

1986

3½ △

C.C.E.'s Tamper Training School

On 8.6.1977 line severed at 2m 65ch. Line on Northampton side of
this point subsequently reinstated as an 'On-track machine training line'

LINE NW051

NORTHAMPTON BRIDGE STREET

1882

LINE N.W.050
'New Line'
Opened 1.8.1881
See page 1

Connections altered early
1903 for new Carriage Shed
See Page 2

LINE N.W.052

To Gas Works
P.S.A. 27.7.1871

0.30

0.27

Duston North Junction S.C.
Opened 3.1899
NW052.012

Duston North Junction S.C.
Opened 1880?
Closed 3.1899
NW052.011

Bridge Street Junction S.C.
Opened 1878
NW051.041

LINE N.W.053
Curve opened 10.8.1880

CANAL

UNION

GRAND

RIVER

NENE

DOWN

UP MAIN

¼

LINE N.W.052

Engine Shed
Opened 1881

T.T. 42 ft

4½

4½

Phipps' Wagon Works Siding

Private Line

Duston West Junction S.C.
Opened 1879
NW051.031

Bridge Street No. 1 S.C.
Closed 1882 and all connections
with Main Lines altered to layout
shown on diagram below
NW051.044

Coal Wharf

C.P.s

G.S.

Former Engine Shed
Erected mid-1850s
Enlarged 1870
Closed 1881

4½

DOWN MAIN

UP MAIN

L.C.

4¾

Bridge Street No. 2 S.C.
NW051.047

1899

Bridge Street Junction S.C.
NW051.041

Bridge Street Junction Frame
Brought into use 10.1882
NW051.043

New 60 ft T.T. installed 1938 and sidings altered
See next page

Engine Shed

Connection severed
between 1923 and 1938

Duston West Junction S.C.
NW051.031

P.S.A. 25.3.1907 Executors of Pickering Phipps
P.S.A. 2.3.1914 to Crown Foundry Co.

Wagon Works

Added by 1924

Coal Wharf

C.P.s

G.S.

4½

DOWN MAIN

UP MAIN

Permanent Way Stores

Sidings further extended by 1938

4¾

L.C.

Added 1914
(See page 12)

Bridge Street Level Crossing S.C.
New S.C. 1907
NW051.048

NORTHAMPTON BRIDGE STREET

1961

A — removed 4.1964, subsequently reinstated, t.o.u. 10.8.1969
B — ✕ t.o.u. 14.9.1964
C — ⊙ t.o.u. unknown dates
D — ⊙ Two sidings t.o.u. 15.8.1969. Major alterations to running lines on 10.8.1969, see below for new layout.

Roade to
Northampton
LINE N.W.080
(See page 1)

Gas Works
Connection t.o.u. c.1970

Br. 3

Duston North Junction S.C.
0.30
Closed 14.7.1970
NW052.012

Bridge Street Junction S.C.
4.23
NW051.041

Down Sidings Frame
4.34
(renewed 1.1950)
NW051.043

Coal Yard

Junction
4.29

BRIDGE STREET STATION
4.52
Closed 4.5.1964

Goods Shed

C.P.s

Bridge Street Level Crossing S.C.
4.56
Reduced to G.F. 10.8.1969
NW051.048

L.C.

4¾ ▽

DOWN MAIN
UP MAIN

A

4½ △

TOP YARD SIDINGS

1
2
3
4

Br. 7B

4¼

Coal Hoist

ENGINE SHED

Ash Plant

T.T. 60 ft

Engine Shed modernised 1952
Closed 27.9.1965
Sidings t.o.u. by 1969

LINE NW052
Curve closed 6.1.1969
t.o.u. 23.2.1969

Br. 2

¼ △

Br. 1

GRAND UNION CANAL

Bridge 7A (Blisworth line)
= Bridge 18 (Roade line)

Line from Blisworth closed 6.1.1969
Down line t.o.u. on 23.2.1969 from crossover at
4¼ M.P. on 4.1.1969. Up line retained
as a shunting neck to 'X'.

Duston West Junction S.C.
3.79 65.09 on H.L.
Closed 23.2.1969
Low level frame closed 23.2.1969
Frame at High Level converted to G.F. 13/15.2.1965
S.C. t.o.u. and new G.F. for High Level opened 10.1969
See also page 1

3.76 = 0.00

DOWN MAIN
UP MAIN

4

NW051.031

1970

1970

D.H.L.B's
9.7.1972

L.C.

4¾ ▽

Bridge Street Level Crossing Frame
4.56
Reinstated as S.C. 18.5.1973
NW051.048

Cattle Dock siding t.o.u. 25.7.1977 (? which)

Bridge Street Crossing G.F.
Brought into use 14/18.5.1973
NW051.046

Sidings — ✕✕ t.o.u. 5.11.1973   R.C.E.   G.F.
NW051.045

C.P.s

Altered layout of running lines brought into use 10.8.1969
(Note altered direction of 'Up')
Siding connection t.o.u. 23/27.4.1973 and facing points laid in Up line.
Line singled (6).5.1973 using Down line.
New connection — brought into use and single line slewed into former Up line 14.18.5.1973

Bridge Street Junction S.C.
4.23
Closed 14.18.5.1973
New G.F. brought into use on same date.
NW051.041

G.F.

UP
DOWN

DOWN
UP   THROUGH SIDING

G.F.

DOWN SIDING No 1

4½ △

SHUNTING NECK

Br. 7B

4½ △

New south approach road
bridge built early 1986

t.o.u. by 5.1986
NW051.042

Siding slewed into through siding 17.10.1984 (✕ t.o.u. ✛✛ new)
and new R.C.E. G.F. brought into use
Siding ⊙—⊙ removed by 5.1986 and two sidings shortened by 70 yds each.

Airflow Streamlines L.C.
(A.O.C.L.)
Brought into use 30.10.1972

Ground Frame

Engineers on track machine
training line

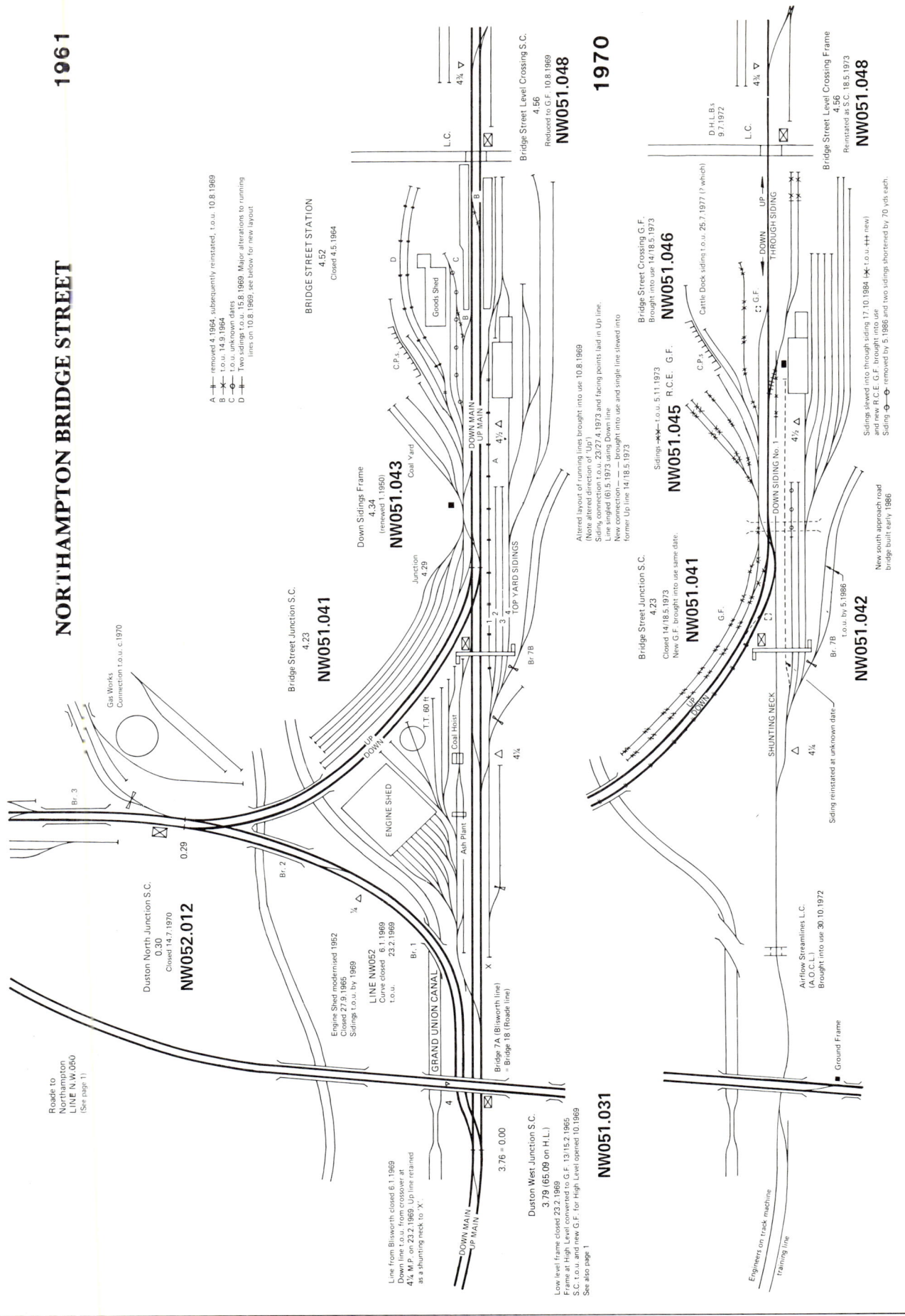

Siding reinstated at unknown date.

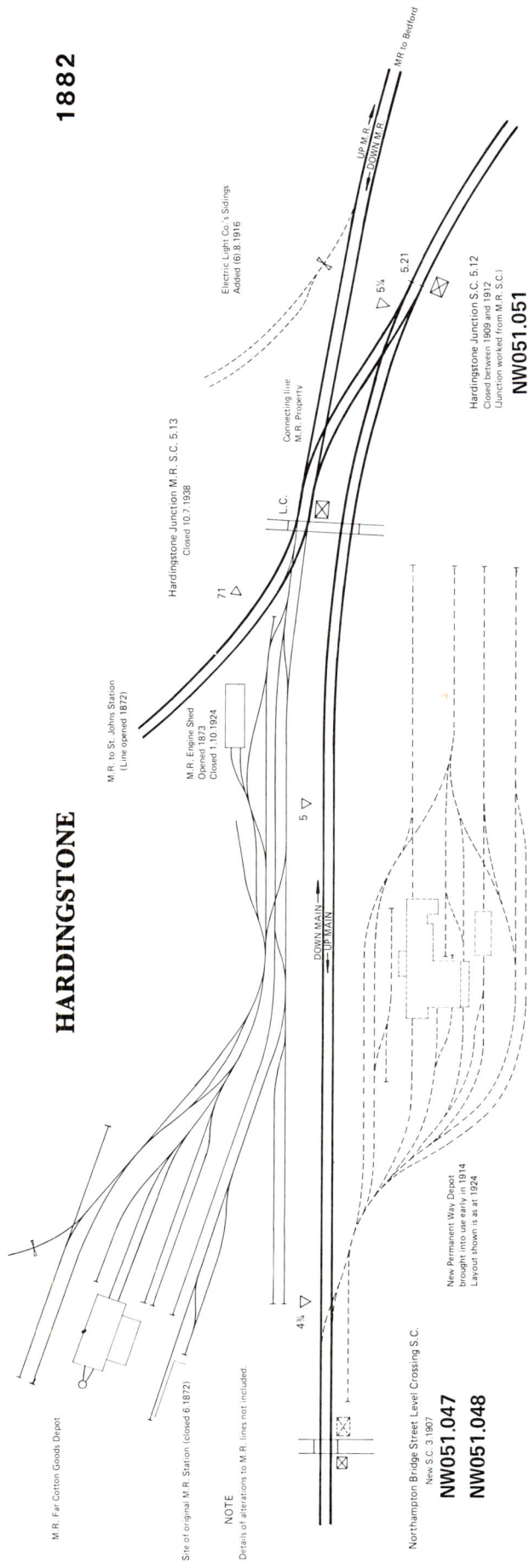

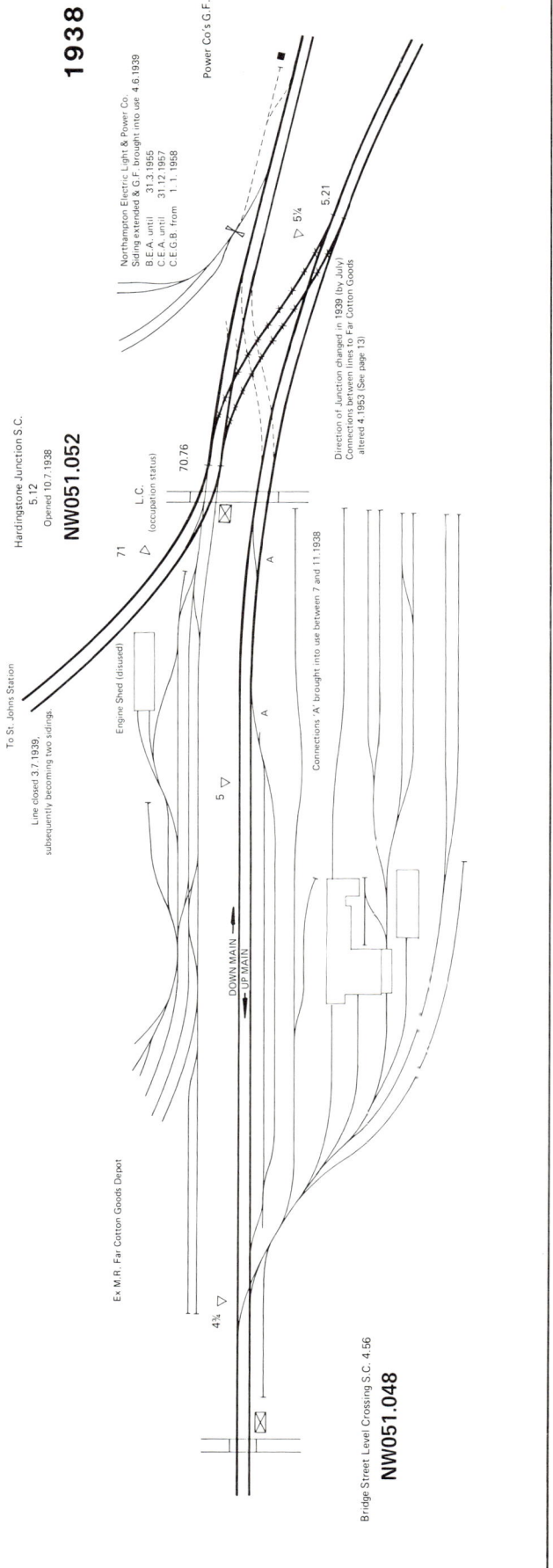

HARDINGSTONE

1882

M R to Bedford

UP M.R
DOWN M.R

Electric Light Co.'s Sidings
Added (6) 8.1916

5.21

Connecting line
M.R. Property

Hardingstone Junction M.R. S.C. 5.13
Closed 10.7.1938

Hardingstone Junction S.C. 5.12
Closed between 1909 and 1912
(Junction worked from M.R.S.C.)

NW051.051

L.C.

71

M.R. to St. Johns Station
(Line opened 1872)

M.R. Engine Shed
Opened 1873
Closed 1.10.1924

5

DOWN MAIN
UP MAIN

M.R. Far Cotton Goods Depot

Site of original M.R. Station (closed 6.1872)

NOTE
Details of alterations to M.R. lines not included.

Northampton Bridge Street Level Crossing S.C.
New S.C. 3.1907

NW051.047
NW051.048

New Permanent Way Depot
brought into use early in 1914
Layout shown is as at 1924

4¾

1938

Power Co's G.F.

Northampton Electric Light & Power Co
Siding extended & G.F. brought into use 4.6.1939
B.E.A. until   31.3.1955
C.E.A. until   31.12.1957
C.E.G.B. from   1.1.1958

5.21

Direction of Junction changed in 1939 (by July)
Connections between lines to Far Cotton Goods
altered 4.1953 (See page 13)

Hardingstone Junction S.C.
5.12
Opened 10.7.1938

NW051.052

L.C.
(occupation status)

70.76

71

To St. Johns Station

Line closed 3.7.1939,
subsequently becoming two sidings.

Engine Shed (disused)

A

A

A

5

DOWN MAIN
UP MAIN

Ex M R Far Cotton Goods Depot

Connections 'A' brought into use between 7 and 11.1938

Bridge Street Level Crossing S.C. 4.56

NW051.048

4¾

HARDINGSTONE

1961

Line singled 10.8.1969 t.o.u.
Portion to right of 'A' subsequently reinstated as siding

See page 11

Far Cotton Goods Yard
Details of alterations not shown

Welding School

St. John's Sidings

Sidings removed (4) 5.1969

Hardingstone Junction S.C. 5.12 = 70.78
Closed 31.5.1970

NW051.052

C.E.G.B.
Power Station Sidings

Power Station closed
'Northampton Rail & Grain Depot' by 1984
Bedford line closed to Passengers 5.3.1962
Bedford line closed to Goods beyond Piddington 20.1.1964
Bedford line singled by 1969
Leased to, and worked by, M.o.D. from 1.3.1968
(as far as Yardley Chase O.E.S.D. Siding)

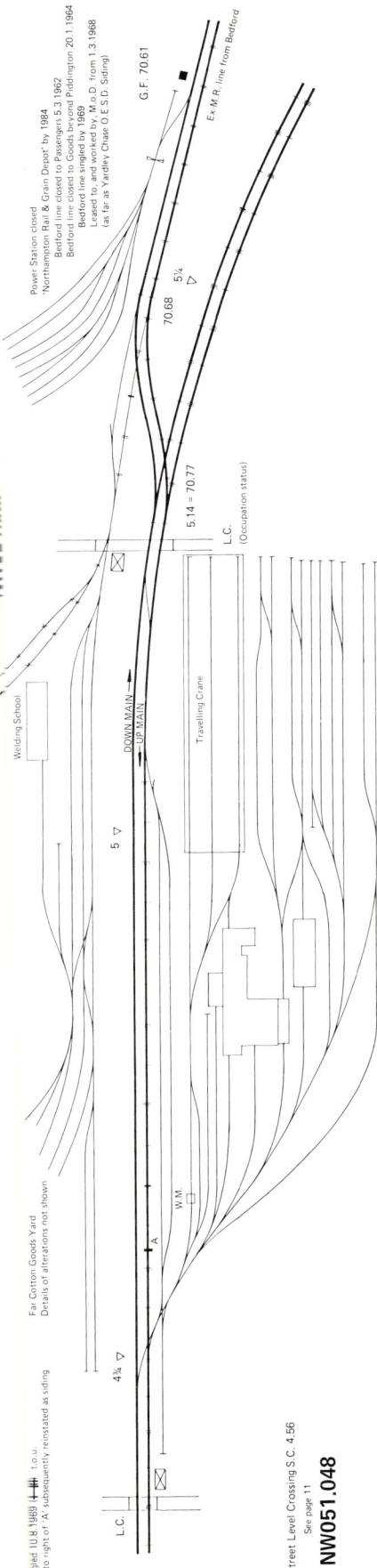

G.F. 70.61

Ex-M.R. line from Bedford

70.68   5¾ ▽

5.14 = 70.77

5.14 = 70.77
L.C.
(Occupation status)

Line to Wellingborough closed   1.8.1966
                      t.o.u.   21.8.1966
Both lines reinstated as sidings for about ⅓M. from junction by 1969
Former Up Up Line shortened to 719 yds from crossover 11.1973

DOWN MAIN
UP MAIN

Travelling Crane

5 ▽

C.C.E.'s Dept. pre-assembly depot

4¾ ▽

A
W.M.

Bridge Street Level Crossing S.C. 4.56
NW051.048

L.C.

LINE NW051 HARDINGSTONE TO WELLINGBOROUGH
Closed to Passengers 4.5.1964
Closed completely 1.8.1966 and t.o.u. 21.8.1966

BEDFORD ROAD

Bedford Road Crossing Frame
6.21
Brought into use 1900
Closed 21.8.1966
NW051.061

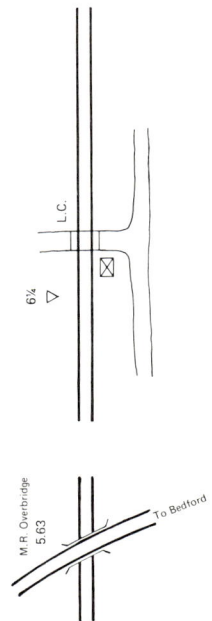

L.C.

6¾ ▽

M.R. Overbridge
5.63

To Bedford

LITTLE HOUGHTON SIDING

1899

Private road to mill

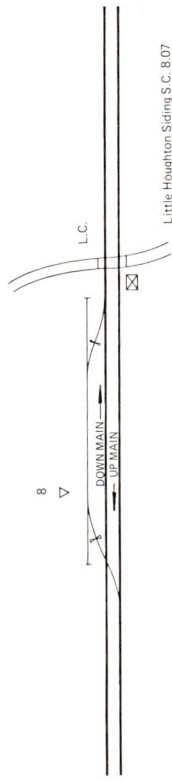

L.C.

Little Houghton Siding S.C. 8.07
Opened 11.1895

NW051.071

8 ▽

DOWN MAIN
UP MAIN

S.C. and siding brought into use 11.1895
Siding t.o.u., S.C. reduced to G.F. controlling L.C. only
and renamed 'Little Houghton Crossing' by 1905
G.F. removed 1957 or 1958

BILLING

1884

1899

Station called 'BILLING ROAD' until 1.4.1883

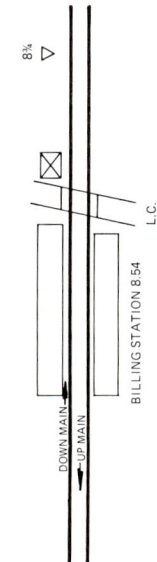

G.F. 8.68 approx.
Brought into use 6.1886
NW051.083

Apparently there was one short siding connected with the Up line by 1886
New Sidings (as below) completed 7.1886

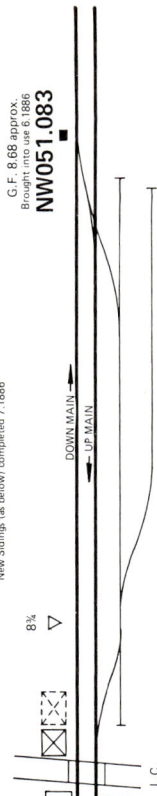

8¾ ▷

8¾ ▷

DOWN MAIN

UP MAIN

DOWN MAIN

UP MAIN

L.C.

L.C.

8.54

BILLING STATION 8.54

BILLING STATION

Closed to Goods 1.6.1964
Sidings t.o.u. 7.9.1964

Billing S.C. 8.57
Opened between 1880 and 1884
NW051.081

Billing S.C. 8.57
New S.C. 2.1908
Closed 21.8.1966
NW051.082

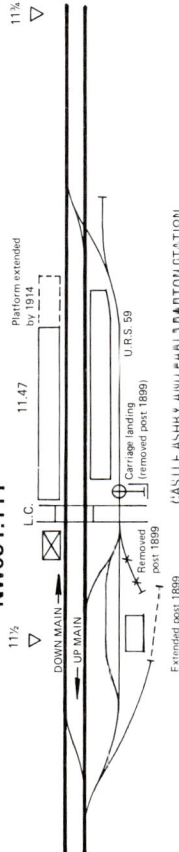

BILLING STATION
Closed to Passengers 6.10.1952
Closed to Goods 1.6.1964

COGENHOE

1884

WHISTON

1915

Lodge

10¾ ▷

DOWN MAIN

UP MAIN

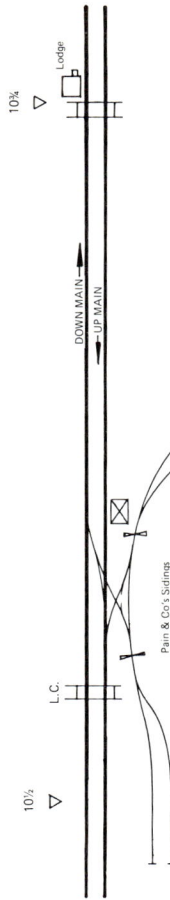

Whiston L.C. 10.60
NW051.102

L.C.

Whiston Sidings S.C. 10.49
Opened 5.8.1914
Closed between 1919 and 1931
NW051.101

Pain & Co's Sidings

Cogenhoe L.C. 9.61
NW051.091

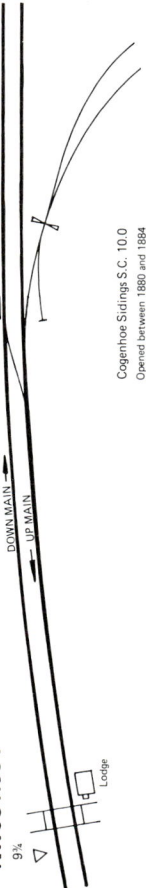

9¾ ▷

10 ▷

DOWN MAIN

UP MAIN

L.C.

To Quarries
Mining commenced 1858
Closure auction held 16.7.1888

Lodge

Cogenhoe Sidings S.C. 10.0
Opened between 1880 and 1884
Closed by 1895
NW051.092

Whiston Ironstone Co. Ltd (Part of J.W. Pain)
P.S.A. 7.11.1914 J. W. Pain Ironstone Mines
Bloxham & Whiston Ironstone Co. w.e.f. 22.12.1917
Quarry closed 1921

10½ ▷

CASTLE ASHBY

1884

1914

Station called CASTLE ASHBY (WHITE MILL)
Renamed CASTLE ASHBY AND EARLS BARTON 5.1869
This layout brought into use 7.1878

Castle Ashby S.C. 11.43
Opened 6.1878
Closed 21.8.1966
NW051.111

11½ ▷

11¾ ▷

11¾ ▷

DOWN MAIN

UP MAIN

DOWN MAIN

UP MAIN

L.C.

Platform extended
by 1914

U.R.S. 59

Br. 15

11.47

Carriage landing
(removed post 1899)

Removed
post 1899

Extended post 1899

CASTLE ASHBY AND EARLS BARTON STATION
Closed to Passengers 4.5.1964
Closed to Goods 1.2.1965

Ropeway
Erected 1913

Tip

Sidings Added 1914
P.S.A. 15.12.1913
Earls Barton Iron Ore Co. Ltd
Quarry closed 1921
Sidings later removed

'Connection from through siding to up shunt neck' t.o.u. 28.4.1963

All remaining connections, except west crossover, t.o.u. 15.5.1966

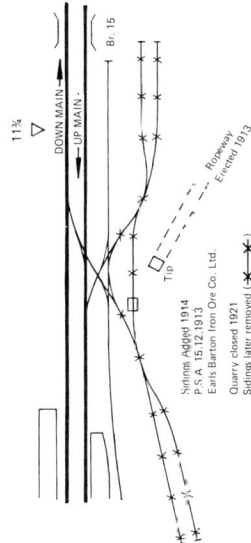

Harrlwater Crossing S.C. 13.18
Opened 4.1899
Closed 19.7.1964 (A.H.B.s)
NW061.121

L.C. ▷ 13¾

Doddington L.C. 14.01
NW051.131

Lodge

Line from Hardingstone Junction to Wellingborough closed 1.8.1966
All remaining lines on this page taken out of use 21.8.1966

WELLINGBOROUGH

1946

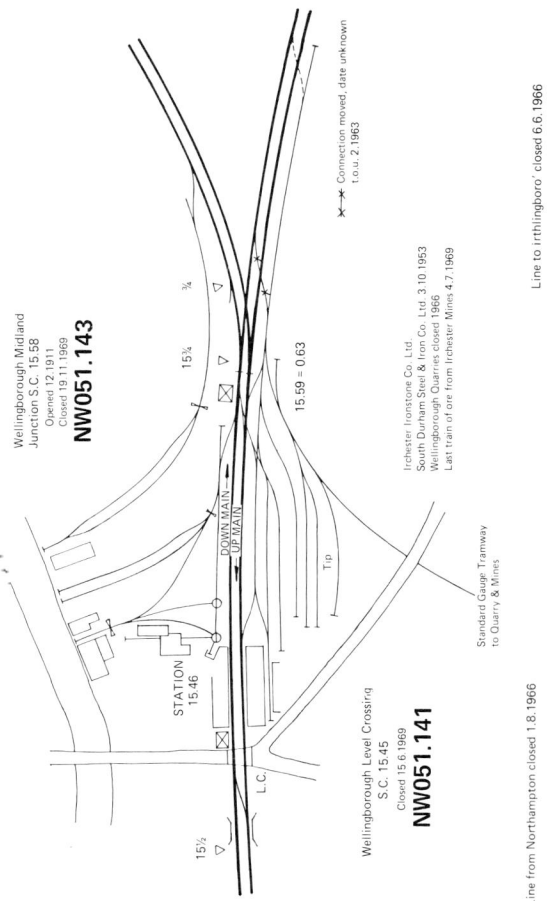

Wellingborough Midland
Junction S.C. 15.58
Opened 12.1911
Closed 19.11.1969
NW051.143

Connection moved, date unknown
t.o.u. 2.1963

15.59 = 0.63

Irchester Ironstone Co. Ltd.
South Durham Steel & Iron Co. Ltd. 3.10.1953
Wellingborough Quarries closed 1966
Last train of ore from Irchester Mines 4.7.1969

STATION
15.46

Standard Gauge Tramway
to Quarry & Mines

Wellingborough Level Crossing
S.C. 15.45
Closed 15.6.1969
NW051.141

Tip

Line to Irthlingboro' closed 6.6.1966

BUTLIN'S SIDING

1884

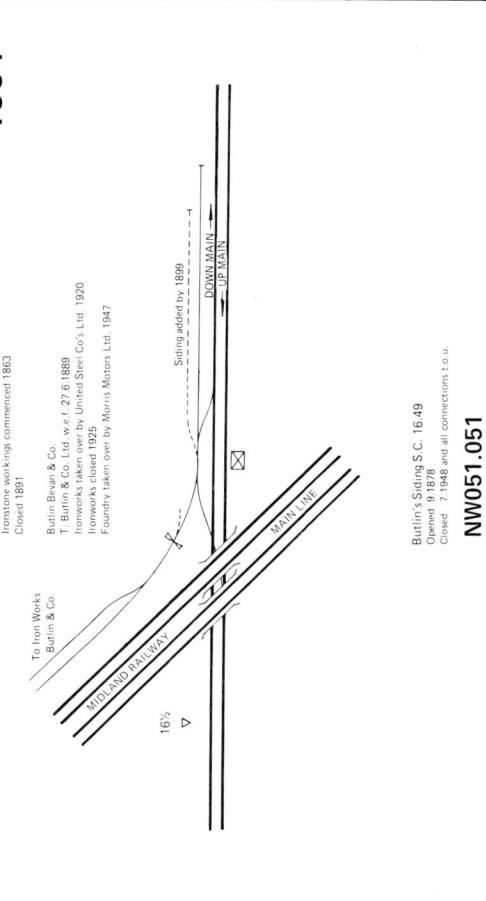

Ironstone workings commenced 1863
Closed 1891

Butlin Bevan & Co.
T. Butlin & Co. Ltd. w.e.f. 27.6.1889
Ironworks taken over by United Steel Co's Ltd 1920
Ironworks closed 1925
Foundry taken over by Morris Motors Ltd. 1947

To Iron Works
Butlin & Co.

Siding added by 1899

DOWN MAIN
UP MAIN

MIDLAND RAILWAY

MAIN LINE

16½

Butlin's Siding S.C. 16.49
Opened 9.1878
Closed 7.1948 and all connections t.o.u.
NW051.051

Line from Northampton closed 1.8.1966

WELLINGBOROUGH

1884

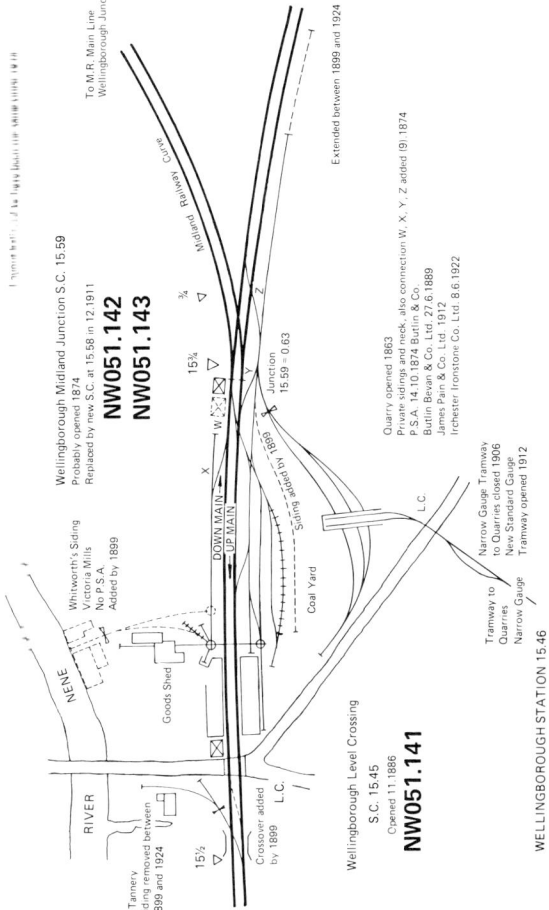

To M.R. Main Line
Wellingborough Junction

Wellingborough Midland Junction S.C. 15.59
Probably opened 1874
Replaced by new S.C. at 15.58 in 12.1911
NW051.142
NW051.143

Midland Railway Curve

Extended between 1899 and 1924

Whitworth's Siding
Victoria Mills
No P.S.A.
Added by 1899

DOWN MAIN
UP MAIN

Junction
15.59 = 0.63

Quarry opened 1863
Private sidings and neck, also connection W, X, Y, Z added (9) 1874
P.S.A. 14.10.1874 Butlin & Co.
Butlin Bevan & Co. Ltd. 27.6.1889
James Pain & Co. Ltd. 1912
Irchester Ironstone Co. Ltd. 8.6.1922

NENE

Goods Shed

Coal Yard

L.C.

Narrow Gauge Tramway
to Quarries closed 1906
New Standard Gauge
Tramway opened 1912

Tramway to
Quarries
Narrow Gauge

RIVER

? Tannery
Siding removed between
1899 and 1924

Crossover added
by 1899

Wellingborough Level Crossing
S.C. 15.45
Opened 11.1886
NW051.141

L.C.

15½

WELLINGBOROUGH STATION 15.46

Renamed Wellingborough, London Road 2.6.1924

Closed to Passengers   4.5.1964
Closed to Goods   7.11.1966 (except private siding)

1970

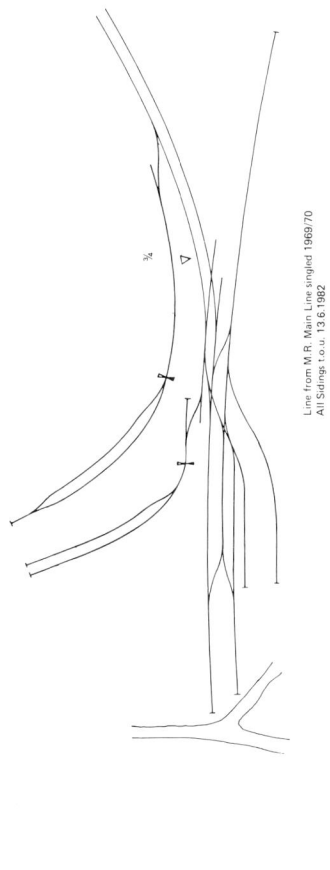

Line from M.R. Main Line singled 1969/70
All Sidings t.o.u. 13.6.1982

LINE NW051

LINE NW051 Line from Northampton to Yarwell Jc. closed to Passengers 4.5.1964
Line from Irthlingborough to Thrapston closed completely 7.6.1965
Line from Wellingborough to Irthlingborough closed completely 6.6.1966

DITCHFORD   1899

NW051.162

G.F. installed 1889
G.F.

17¾
△

Later site of G.F.

NW051.161

UP MAIN
DOWN MAIN
17.57
G.F.
L.C.

DITCHFORD STATION
Closed to Passengers 1.11.1924
Siding added (23) 1.1889
Extended between 1899 and 1924
P.S.A. 6.6.1917 T. W. Ward
(?) second siding at this date
Closed 15.5.1950, removed 1956

DITCHFORD   1875

RIXON'S & WHITEHOUSE'S SIDING

Thomas Whitehouse
Quarry opened 1873
Thrapston Iron Ore Co 1875
Butlin Bevan & Co. 1879
Quarry closed 1885

Siding for Rixon & Co.
Added 1878 (completed in May)
Removed between 1884 and 1889

Tramway
Loading Stage
A
B
18 △
DOWN MAIN
UP MAIN
C
D

Whitehouse's Siding S.C.
Opened 11.1875
Closed 5.1878

Rixon's Siding S.C.
Opened 5.1877
Closed 5.1878

Rixon & Whitehouse's Siding S.C. 17.78
Opened 5.1878
Probably closed 1887

As a result of the Board of Trade inspection of the signalling arrangements when Rixon's Siding was opened in 1877, the two cabins were replaced by one central cabin in May 1878. At the same time, connection A moved to B, connection C moved to D.

NW051.163   NW051.164   NW051.165

DITCHFORD   1899

'New Ironstone Sidings for Mr. Whitehouse'
Added 1875 (completed in December)
Removed between 1884 and 1889

17¾ △
RIVER NENE
L.C.
DITCHFORD STATION
17.57

HIGHAM FERRERS & IRTHLINGBOROUGH   1899

Originally HIGHAM FERRERS.
Renamed HIGHAM FERRERS & IRTHLINGBOROUGH 28.4.1885
Renamed IRTHLINGBOROUGH 1.10.1910

NW051.173

G.F.
? position

DOWN MAIN
UP MAIN
G.S
× removed, date unknown
20 △
L.C.

STATION 20.00
Closed to Passengers 4.5.1964
Closed to Goods 6.6.1966

Higham Ferrers S.C. 19.78
Opened 2.1887
Closed 6.6.1966

NW051.172

IRTHLINGBORO IRON ORE SIDING   1899

Dunmore Ltd. had a brickworks here. Closed 1908
Site worked by Hatton, Shaw & Co. (Irthlingborough) Ltd.
as a tannery. Traffic worked by Ebbw Vale Co. after 1915.

Cement Works Siding, added 1897
P.S.A. 6.8.1897 A. Dunmore
P.S.A. 8.4.1904 A. Dunmore
P.S.A. 23.6.1905 Dunmores Ltd.
At 1905 shown as 'Premier Portland Cement Co. Ltd.'
At 3.1916 used by British Portland Cement Manufacturers Ltd.' only
P.S.A. 14.1.1916 Ebbw Vale Steel & Iron Co. Ltd.
Disused at 1925

Iron Ore Quarries
P.S.A. 28.8.1890 Irthlingboro' Iron Ore Co
P.S.A. 12.1.1911 T. W. Ward Ltd.
Ebbw Vale Iron Ore Quarry opened 1915
Mine opened 1918
Ebbw Vale Steel, Iron & Coal Co. Ltd. c.1925
Richard Thomas & Co. Ltd. 9.11.1935
Richard Thomas & Baldwins Ltd. 3.1.1945
Mine closed 30.9.1965

19 △
NENE
RIVER
DOWN MAIN
UP MAIN
19¼ △
L.C.

Crossover added 1918 (completed on 12 August)

Irthlingboro Iron Ore Co's Siding S.C. 19.12
Opened 11.1890 (as Spencer's Siding?)

NW051.171

RINGSTEAD

1884

Renamed RINGSTEAD AND ADDINGTON 1.4.1898

DOWN MAIN
UP MAIN

L.C.

22½ ▷
23 ▷

22.59

Lever frame installed 2.1887 functioning as signal cabin. Reduced to G.F. between 1949 and 1956.

NW051.181

NW051.182

Private sidings removed by 1899
Remaining public siding closed 2.3.1964
Butlin Bevan & Co.
T. Butlin & Co. Ltd. from 27.6.1889. Closed 1891
RINGSTEAD STATION
Closed to Passengers 4.5.1964
Closed to Goods 2.3.1964

G.F.

Tramway to quarry

NEWBRIDGE SIDING

1884

1884

All sidings removed between 1895 and 1899

Tramway to quarry

DOWN MAIN
UP MAIN

22½ ▷
23½ ▷

Woodford Mill

Newbridge Sidings S.C. 23.30
Opened 10.1873
Closed 1896/1899

NW051.183

RIVER
NENE

Viaduct 23.11
107 yds approx.

23¾ ▷
23.54
93 yds approx.

Viaduct 23.54

RIVER
NENE

Woodford Mill L.C. (?)

NW051.201

Lodge
Mill
L.C.

RIVER
NENE

Viaduct 97 yds Approx.

WOODFORD SIDING

1884

DOWN MAIN
UP MAIN

24 ▷

'Siding for Mr. Butlin' installed 1884 (completed in July)
Removed by 1899

Woodford Sidings S.C. 24.01
Opened 6.1884
Closed by 1896

NW051.191

KEEBLES SIDING

1916

DOWN MAIN
UP MAIN

24 ▷

Tip

Keebles Siding S.C. 23.77 approx
Opened (26).11.1912
Closed between 1919 and 1931

NW051.192

Keeble & Jellett Ironstone Sidings
R.E. Campbell from 1914
Ebbw Vale Steel, Iron & Coal Co. Ltd. from 1916
Quarry closed 1917 or 1918
P.S.A. 23.9.1912 Keeble & Jellett
P.S.A. 14.1.1916 Ebbw Vale Co.

ISLIP IRON ORE SIDING

To Iron Works
Islip Iron Co. from 1873
Islip Iron Co. Ltd. 8.8.1903
Stewarts & Lloyds Ltd. from 1932
Stewarts & Lloyds Minerals Ltd. 1.1.1950

Added by 1909

Sidings brought into use 1.1886
Originally only two private sidings
(Positions not known)

P.S.A. 10.4.1889 Islip Iron Co.
Later Stewarts and Lloyds

Sidings subsequently extended?

25¼ ▷
25¾ ▷

Islip Iron Co's Siding S.C. 25.34
Opened 12.1886

NW051.211

Viaduct 25.47
97 yds approx.

MIDLAND RAILWAY
To Kettering
From Huntingdon

THRAPSTON

1899

Renamed THRAPSTON BRIDGE STREET 2.6.1924
Believed that the down platform was south of the L.C. prior to 1886

DOWN MAIN
UP MAIN

25.62
25¾ ▷

Thrapston No. 1 S.C. 25.60
Opened 9.1886

NW051.221

Thrapston No. 2 G.F.
Opened 1886
Later replaced by open G.F.s?
Position not known

NW051.222

Down Sidings Frame

NW051.223

Up Sidings Frame

NW051.224

Crossover replaced by slip (date unknown)

Removed, date unknown

G.S.

L.C.

THRAPSTON STATION
Closed to Passengers 4.5.1964
Closed to Goods 7.6.1965

RIVER
NENE

Line to Oundle closed completely 4.5.1964

LINE NW051

Line from Irthlingborough closed 7.6.1965 and all remaining L.N.W. lines on this page closed.

THORPE — 1872 / 1880 / 1899

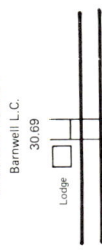

Barnwell L.C. 30.69
NW051.251
Lodge
G.F. (? Position)

Wigsthorpe L.C. 30.01
NW051.241
Lodge
G.F. (? Position)

THORPE STATION
Closed to Passengers and Goods 4.5.1964
Thorpe S.C. 28.28
Opened 12.1880
NW051.231

Connections altered 1.1888
28½
G.F. (? position)
NW051.232
DOWN MAIN
UP MAIN
28.30
L.C.

Station buildings moved to Wansford 1977

BARNWELL — 1899

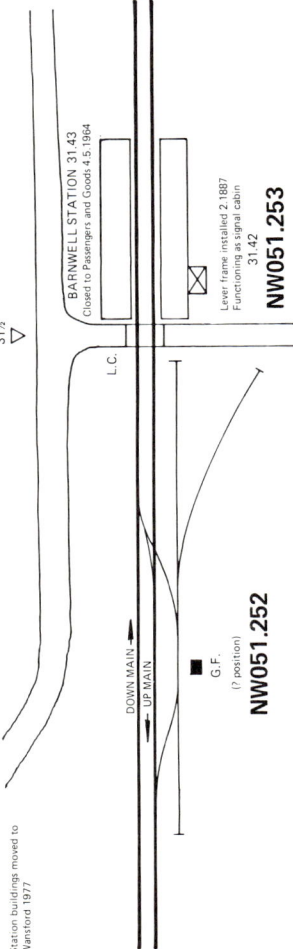

Gipsy Lane L.C. 32.77
NW051.262
33

All sidings removed by 1885
DOWN MAIN
UP MAIN

Oundle Ballast Pit S.C. (? Name)
Opened c.9.1872
Closed by 1885
NW051.261

Viaduct 32.60 approx.
NENE RIVER

OUNDLE BALLAST PIT

BARNWELL STATION 31.43
Closed to Passengers and Goods 4.5.1964
Lever frame installed 2.1887
Functioning as signal cabin
31.42
NW051.253

31½
L.C.

Oundle No. 1 S.C. 34.0
Opened 6.1887
NW051.271
G.F. (? position)
NW051.252

Viaduct 33.71
93 yds approx.

OUNDLE — 1899

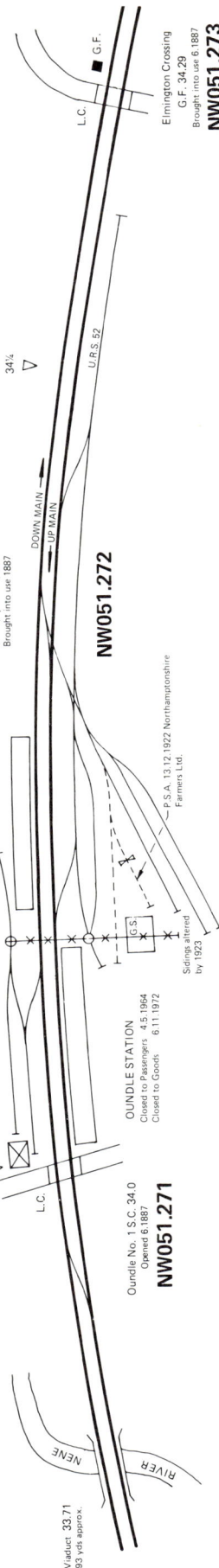

Elmington Crossing
G.F. 34.29
Brought into use 6.1887
NW051.273
L.C.
G.F.

34¼

DOWN MAIN
UP MAIN
U.R.S. 52

Oundle No. 2 G.F.
(? position)
Brought into use 1887
NW051.272

P.S.A. 13.12.1922 Northamptonshire Farmers Ltd.

G.S.
Sidings altered by 1923

OUNDLE STATION
Closed to Passengers 4.5.1964
Closed to Goods 6.11.1972

34
L.C.

ELTON — 1884 / 1876

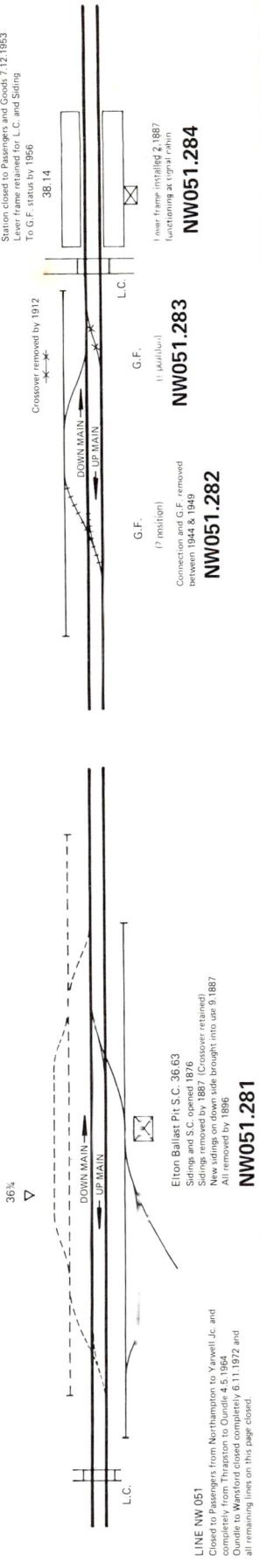

ELTON STATION
Station closed to Passengers and Goods 7.12.1953
Lever frame retained for L.C. and Siding
To G.F. status by 1956
38.14
NW051.284

Lever frame installed 2.1887
(functioning as signal cabin)
NW051.284
L.C.

Crossover removed by 1912

DOWN MAIN
UP MAIN
G.F.
G.F. (? position)

Connection and G.F. removed between 1944 & 1949
NW051.282
NW051.283

ELTON BALLAST PIT

Elton Ballast Pit S.C. 36.63
Sidings and S.C. opened 1876
Sidings removed by 1887 (Crossover retained)
New sidings on down side brought into use 9.1887
All removed by 1896
NW051.281

36¾
DOWN MAIN
UP MAIN
L.C.

LINE NW 051
Closed to Passengers from Northampton to Yarwell Jc. and completely from Thrapston to Oundle 4.5.1964
Oundle to Wansford closed completely 6.11.1972 and all remaining lines on this page closed.

WANSFORD

YARWELL JUNCTION

1875

Stamford and Essendine Rly
Opened 9.8.1867

SIBSON PLATFORM

Junction with S & E Railway severed 1.1.1870 after a dispute
Junction reinstated early in 1878

NW051.305

L.C. Frame
NW051.302

Goods Shed

L.C.

40½

39¾

Contractors siding and temporary signal cabin
brought into use 1878

NW051.291

DOWN MAIN
UP MAIN

1887

G.N.R. (ex S & E) to Stamford
Closed 1.7.1929
t.o.u. 11.10.1930

Wansford S.C. 40.56
Opened 4.1.1907
NW051.304

Viaduct 80 yds approx.
40.58

RIVER NENE
40.62

Wansford No. 3 S.C. 40.62
G.N. Junction
New S.C. 1907
Closed 1907
NW051.306

Wansford No. 2 S.C. 40.55
Opened 2.1879
Closed 1907
NW051.303

L.C.
Great North Road

Removed by 1899
Added by 1900
t.o.u. 11.10.1930

G.S.

Wansford No. 1 S.C. 40.44
Opened 2.1879
Closed 1907
NW051.301

Layout altered 1907
×—× t.o.u.
-—- new

DOWN MAIN
UP MAIN

40½

39¾

LINE N.W.056
From Seaton, Opened 21.7.1879
See page 33

Yarwell Junction S.C. 39.54
Opened 3.1.1879
Closed 3.1.1879
NW051.291

1931

Wansford S.C. 40.56
Closed 30.3.1971
NW051.304

Portion of Up Line removed (26) 2.1967
Remainder of line from Peterborough
became a tamper training line
Down line became single line

Wansford S.C. 40.56
Closed 30.3.1971
NW051.304

L.C.

40½

Removed by 1967

G.S.

WANSFORD STATION 40.51
Closed to Passengers 1.7.1967
Closed to Goods 13.7.1964
Sidings removed by 1971

New overbridge
for A1 road 1959

D.R.S. 24

Two single lines
from (1.1.1967)

DOWN MAIN
UP MAIN

40.27

40½

39¾

For details of closure of line from
Seaton see page 33
Line from Kingscliffe singled (1.1.1967?)

Line from Oundle singled (1.1.1967?)
Line from Oundle closed 6.11.1972

WANSFORD TUNNEL 619 yds

39.78

Line from Oundle to Fletton Road Junction closed 6.11.1972
and all remaining lines on this page closed
Wansford to Fletton Road Junction retained until 17.2.1976
at least and traversed by Peterborough Railway Society special
train (to and from Nassington — Line N.W.056 — see page 33)

NENE VALLEY RAILWAY
Wansford Station reopened by Nene Valley Railway 4.6.1977 (seasonal)
Full details of N.V.R. activities not included in this book

LINE NW051

CASTOR

1897

NW051.311

Castor Station Frame 41.75 approx.
Opened c.10.1897
Closed 13.8.1966

Siding opened c.26.9.1897

42 ▽

DOWN MAIN

G.F. ■

UP MAIN

Yard G.F.
Opened 1897

NW051.312

CASTOR STATION   41.77 approx.
Closed to Passengers 1.7.1957
Closed to Goods 28.12.1964

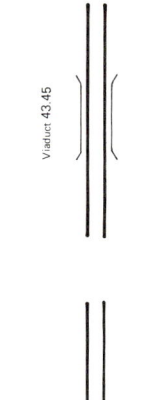

OVERTON

1899

Station renamed ORTON WATERVILLE 1.8.1913

44½ ▽

DOWN MAIN

UP MAIN

Viaduct 43.45

Sidings installed c.4.1878
Removed by 2.1966

C.P.s

OVERTON STATION   44.30
Closed to Passengers 5.10.1942
Closed to Goods 28.12.1964

Overton S.C.   44.28
Opened 2.1878
Closed 13.6.1966

NW051.321

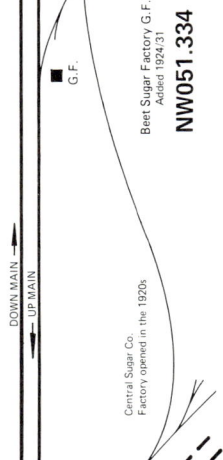

LONGVILLE JUNCTION

1899

1935

45¾ ▽

DOWN MAIN

UP MAIN

45.52

Longville Junction S.C. 45.52
Opened 10.1880
Closed 1929

NW051.332

G.N.R. to Fletton Junction
Curve approved for use 4.1881
Used for diverted L.N.W trains 6.16.12.1881
Opened for Passenger Trains 2.7.1883
Closed 12.1929

46 ▽

45¾ ▽

DOWN MAIN

UP MAIN

Longville G.F. Up Line added 1944/49
Branch reopened 12.1947 for brick trains from Yaxley

NW051.333

Site of
Longville Junction

Central Sugar Co.
Factory opened in the 1920s

Beet Sugar Factory Sidings

G.F. ■

Beet Sugar Factory G.F.
Added 1924/31

NW051.334

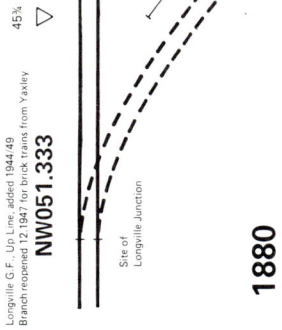

WOODSTONE WHARF

1880

46½ ▽

RIVER   NENE

G.S.

New connecting line added 1885

Woodstone Wharf S.C.
Opened ?
Closed 1885

NW051.341

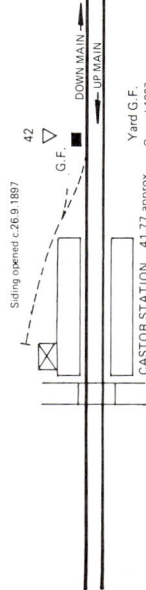

RIVER   NENE

46½ ▽

G.S.

W.M.

D.R.S. 38

46¾ ▽

Woodstone Wharf S.C. 46.58
Opened 10.1885
Closed 20.11.1966

NW051.342

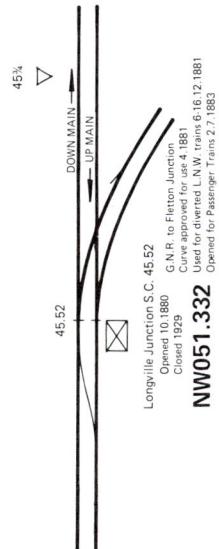

PETERBOROUGH

1899

G.N.R.
To Doncaster

M.R.
From Melton Mowbray

Second viaduct and two additional lines
added on the west side and opened 2.11.1924.

From London

Fletton Road Jc.
G.E.R.
S.C. & L.C. closed 1934

47.08

M.R.   G.E.R.

47 ▽

L.N.W.R.   G.E.R.

46.74

Tank
House

Engine
Shed

T.T.
45

DOWN MAIN

UP MAIN

N E N E

New engine shed and associated sidings
brought into use 9.1885. Locally known
as Water End Shed. Closed 8.2.1932 and
engines and men transferred to ex Midland
shed at Spital Bridge.

First altered (?6).2.1967
Up line converted to
tamper training line.
Down line converted
into single line to Wansford.

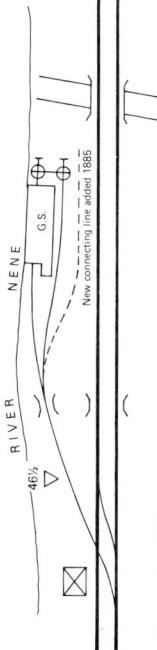

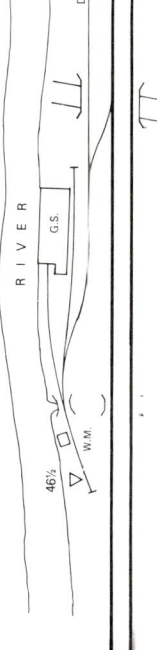

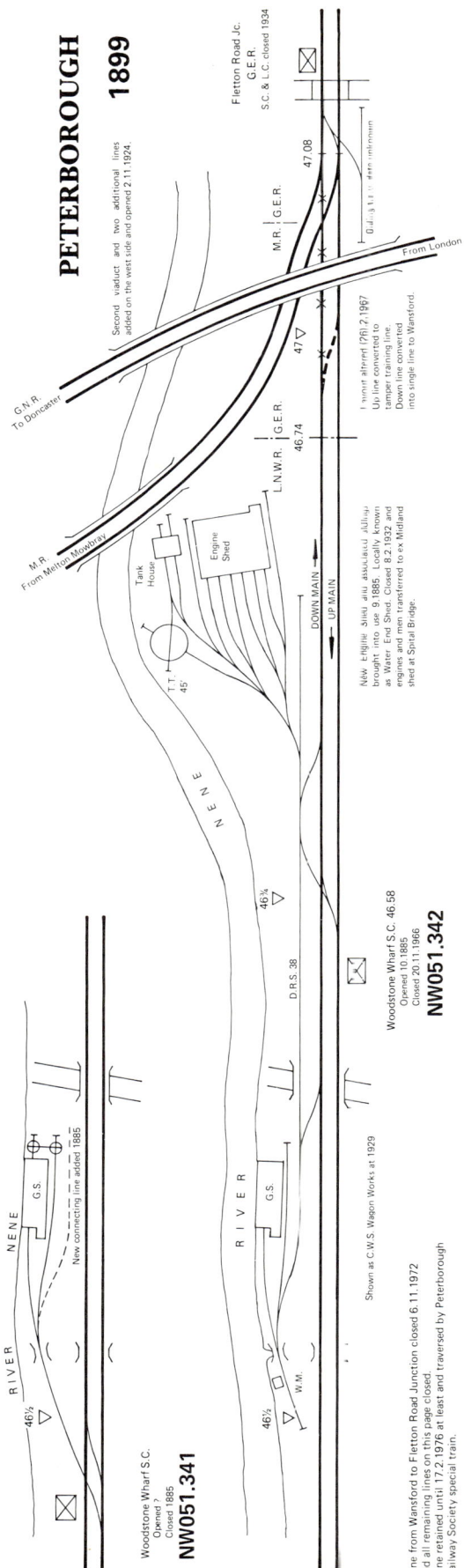

Shown as C.W.S. Wagon Works at 1929

Line from Wansford to Fletton Road Junction closed 6.11.1972
and all remaining lines on this page closed.
Line retained until 17.2.1976 at least and traversed by Peterborough
Railway Society special train.

BOUGHTON CROSSING

1960

1899

Northampton to Yarwell Junction
Local Passenger service withdrawn 4.1.1960

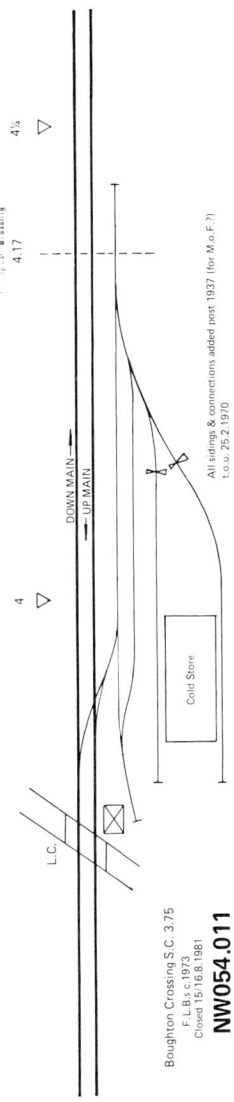

From Northampton
See page 6

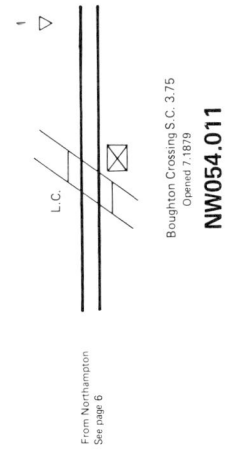

4¾

4.17

L.C.

All sidings & connections added post 1937 (for M.o.F.?)
t.o.u. 25.2.1970

Cold Store

DOWN MAIN
UP MAIN

4

1

L.C.

Boughton Crossing S.C. 3.75
F.L.B.s c.1973
Closed 15/16.8.1981

NW054.011

Boughton Crossing S.C. 3.75
Opened 7.1879

NW054.011

PITSFORD & BRAMPTON

1929

Viaduct 5.15
62 yds approx.

Layout at Pitsford & Brampton the same since 1884

5

Pitsford & Brampton S.C. 4.76
Opened c.1879
Closed 4.10.1965

NW054.022

Crossover t.o.u. 4.10.1965

DOWN MAIN
UP MAIN

4¾

Station originally called PITSFORD
Renamed BRAMPTON & PITSFORD June 1859
Renamed BRAMPTON 1.4.1860
Renamed PITSFORD & BRAMPTON 24.11.1881

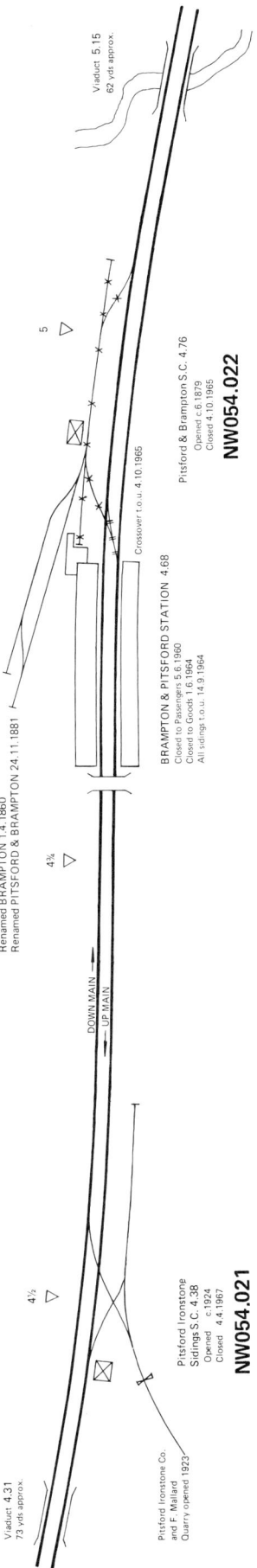

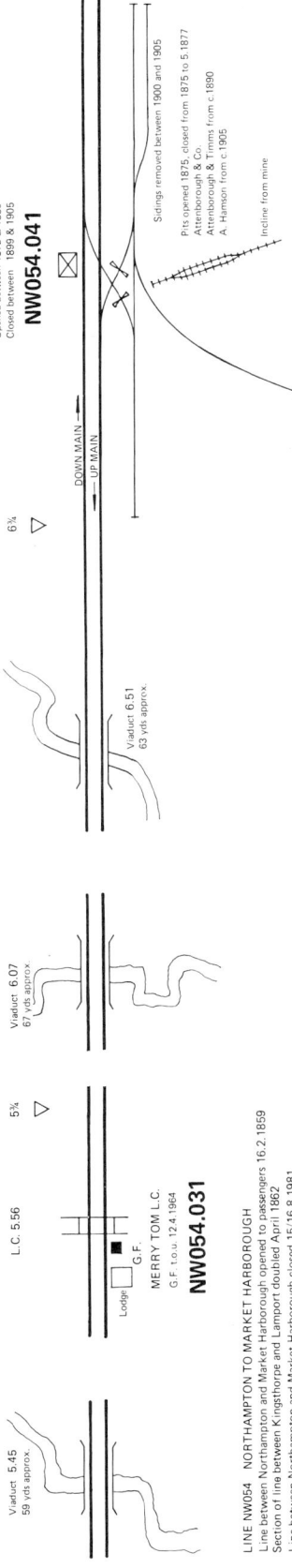

BRAMPTON & PITSFORD STATION 4.68
Closed to Passengers 5.6.1960
Closed to Goods 1.6.1964
All sidings t.o.u. 14.9.1964

PITSFORD IRONSTONE SIDINGS

1899

Viaduct 4.31
73 yds approx.

4½

Pitsford Ironstone
Sidings S.C. 4.38
Opened   c.1924
Closed   4.4.1967

NW054.021

Pitsford Ironstone Co.
and F. Mallard
Quarry opened 1923

ATTENBORO SIDINGS

1899

Attenboro' Sidings S.C. 6.67
Opened between 1872 & 1880
Closed between 1899 & 1905

NW054.041

Sidings removed between 1900 and 1905

Pits opened 1875, closed from 1875 to 5.1877
Attenborough & Co.
Attenborough & Timms from c.1890
A. Hamson from c.1905

Incline from mine

6¾

DOWN MAIN
UP MAIN

Viaduct 6.51
63 yds approx.

Viaduct 6.07
67 yds approx.

MERRY TOM L.C.

L.C. 5.56

5¾

Lodge   G.F.

MERRY TOM L.C.
G.F. t.o.u. 12.4.1964

NW054.031

Viaduct 5.45
59 yds approx.

LINE NW054   NORTHAMPTON TO MARKET HARBOROUGH
Line between Northampton and Market Harborough opened to passengers 16.2.1859
Section of line between Kingsthorpe and Lamport doubled April 1862
Line between Northampton and Market Harborough closed 15/16.8.1981
Renamed Engineers Sidings 27.2.1984

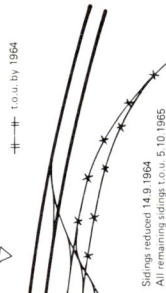

SPRATTON

1924

Spratton S.C. 7.34
Opened 7.1879
Closed 1981

NW054.051

SPRATTON STATION 7.30
Station opened 1.3.1864
Closed to Passengers 23.5.1949

8.10

Br. 18

BRIXWORTH STATION 8.10

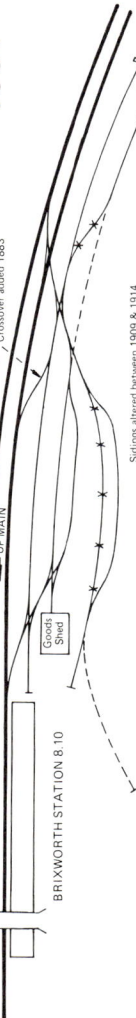

BRIXWORTH

1929

Brixworth S.C. 8.17
Closed 5.10.1965

NW054.061

8¼

DOWN MAIN

UP MAIN

G.S.

BRIXWORTH STATION 8.10
Closed to Passengers 4.1.1960
Closed to Goods 1.6.1964
(except private siding)

t.o.u. by 1964

To quarry

Brixworth Ironstone Co. Ltd. 11.3.1909 (Messrs. Hamon)
Became subsidiary of Clay Cross Co. 1929
Closed 1947, line removed by 1964

Sidings reduced 14.9.1964
All remaining sidings t.o.u. 5.10.1965

1884

Brixworth S.C. 8.17
Opened 7.1879

NW054.061

8¼

DOWN MAIN

UP MAIN

Goods
Shed

Crossover added 1883

Sidings altered between 1909 & 1914
(✕✕✕ removed — — — new)

1913

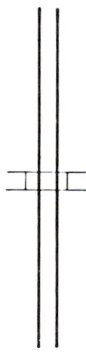

Tramway to Quarry
Pits opened 1863. Rev. C. F. Watkins
Attenborough & Co. from 1872
P.S.A. 6.12.1873 Richard Attenborough & Others
Attenborough & Timms from c.1890

W.M.

LAMPORT IRONSTONE SIDINGS

Lamport Ironstone Sidings S.C. 8.76
Opened   9.1912
Closed   17.2.1970

NW054.071

9

DOWN MAIN

UP MAIN

W.M.

Tip

Sidings added ----- date unknown
Lamport Ironstone Co.
P.S.A. 20.6.1912 Staveley Coal & Iron Co. Ltd.
(Sidings out of use at 1929, later brought back into use)
Staveley Iron & Chemical Co. Ltd. from 21.9.1968

Ropeway from pits replaced by
S.G. line Jan 1955

ISHAM L.C.

Isham L.C. 10.12

NW054.073

Hanging Houghton L.C. 9.44

NW054.072

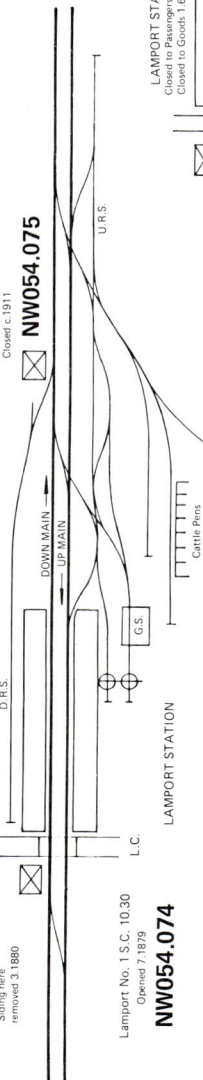

LAMPORT

1913

10½

Crossover t.o.u. 24.2.1970

U.R.S.77

DOWN MAIN

UP MAIN

Goods Shed

Cattle Pens

Closed to Goods 1.6.1964
Yard sidings t.o.u. same date ✕✕✕

LAMPORT STATION
Closed to Passengers 4.1.1960
Closed to Goods 1.6.1964

Lamport L.D.O. 10.00

L.C.
F.L.Bs 11.4.1965

Closed 1981

NW054.074

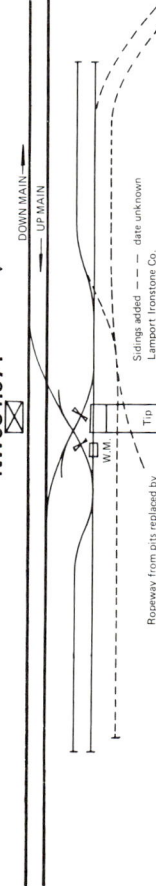

10½

Lamport No. 2 S.C. 10.43
Opened 7.1879
Closed c.1911

NW054.075

DOWN MAIN

UP MAIN

U.R.S.

Cattle Pens

G.S.

LAMPORT STATION

D.R.S.

D.R.S. was originally south of L.C.
L.C. moved 2.1880

Siding here
removed 3.1880

Glendon Iron Co. Quarry opened 1887?
Glendon Iron Co. Ltd. 23.6.1886
Quarry closed 1890

Lamport No. 1 S.C. 10.30
Opened 7.1879

NW054.074

1899

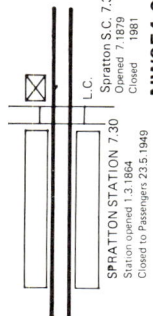

LINE NW054
Line doubled to Market Harborough
Brought into use 4.8.1879
Line closed 15/16.8.1981

DRAUGHTON SIDING

1905

L.C.

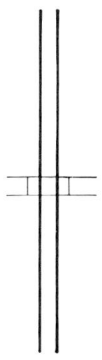

DOWN MAIN →
→ UP MAIN

Draughton Sidings S.C. 11.60
Opened 6.1901
Converted to G.F. between 1919 and 1929
Closed 1 b/16.8.1981

NW054.081

Site of previous S.C. prior
to installation of sidings

P.S.A. 11.3.1900 Stanton Iron Co.
Sidings believed to have been brought into use 1901
Pits abandoned 1920
Sidings removed by 1929

GREEN LANE L.C.

Green Lane L.C. 12.35

NW054.091

KELMARSH

1960

G.F.

Kelmarsh S.C. 14.03
Closed 31.10.1971

NW054.101

14 ▽

KELMARSH STATION

U.R.S. 33

Air Ministry
Petrol Storage Depot

Two sidings removed 18.3.1964

G.F. and connections brought
into use in 1943 or 1944

NW054.102

Sidings ┼┼ removed by 1971
All sidings and connections t.o.u. 28.2.1971

KELMARSH

1899

13.02   13.26

13.78

KELMARSH TUNNELS
518 yds

N.B. Tunnels also given as 531 yds

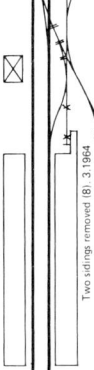

DOWN MAIN
← UP MAIN

U.R.S. 33

14 ▽

KELMARSH STATION 13.78

Kelmarsh S.C. 14.03
Opened 7.1879

NW054.101

LITTLE BOWDEN CROSSING

To Market Harborough
See page 26

F.L.B.'s by 9.1976

L.C.

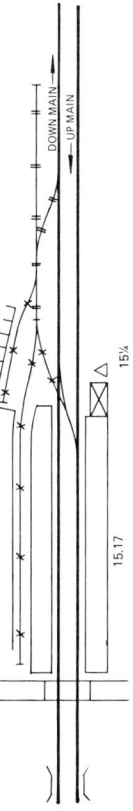

15.53   15.74

462 yds
453 yds

OXENDON TUNNELS

NW054.112

Little Bowden Crossing S.C. 17.74
Opened 7.1879
Closed 15/16.8.1981

NW054.121

CLIPSTON & OXENDON

1899

Station originally called CLIPSTONE & OXENDEN
Opened to Passengers 1.6.1863
Opened to Goods 9.1879
Spelling corrected to CLIPSTON & OXENDON 11.1879

L.C.

Reduced to 'occupation status' 25.8.1970

C.P.'s

15¼

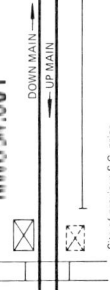

DOWN MAIN
← UP MAIN

Sidings removed by 1969

Prior to doubling there were no sidings here
Public goods facilities opened 9.1879

15.17

CLIPSTON & OXENDON STATION
Closed to Passengers   4.1.1960
Closed to Goods   4.1.1960
Sidings   6.4.1977
┼┼┼ t.o.u.   18.3.1964

NW054.111

Clipston & Oxendon S.C. 15.19
Opened   7.1879
Closed   6.4.1977
Crossover t.o.u. same date
Opened 4.8.1879

LINE NW054
The line between Lamport and Market Harborough was doubled in 1879. Opened 4.8.1879
Line closed 15/16.8.1981

24

CLIFTON MILL

1880

From Rugby
See Line N.W.030
(Section 3)

Loop brought into use 18.8.1888

Up Line diverted 1885 i.c.w.
New Layout at Rugby

CLIFTON MILL STATION

DOWN MAIN
UP MAIN

L.C.

Clifton Mill S.C. 0.75
Opened 12.1878
NW056.021

Siding Frame
NW056.022

Line N.W.056 RUGBY TO YARWELL JUNCTION
Originally single line
Line doubled Rugby to Market Harborough 22.7.1878
Line closed Rugby to Market Harborough 6.6.1966
All lines taken out of use 10.7.1966

1960

Crossover moved 20.12.1963

t.o.u. 7.10.1963

L.C.

S.C.

NW056.021

Line to Market Harborough closed 6.6.1966, all track t.o.u. 10.7.1966
except Down Main retained to 'X' as shunting spur from Rugby, S.C. closed.
Spur subsequently shortened

1903

OXFORD CANAL

CLIFTON MILL ARM (DISUSED)

ENGINE LOOP

DOWN
UP

Line N.W.055

Slip brought into use (17).11.1911

Facing connection removed
between 1929 & 1939

DOWN MAIN
UP MAIN

L.C.

Siding Frame
Removed between 1937 and 1939
(Connections worked from S.C. thereafter)
NW056.022

Siding removed date unknown

S.C. 0.75
Closed 10.7.1966

CLIFTON MILL STATION 0.73
Closed to Passengers 6.4.1953
Closed to Goods 6.4.1953
NW056.021

Note: The Engine Loop became a Down Goods Line from c.1938 to c.1950
Known as Down Peterborough Goods

LILBOURNE

1885

LILBOURNE STATION 3.43
Closed to Passengers 6.6.1966

Lilbourne S.C. 3.41
Opened 12.1878
Reduced to G.F. between 1919 and 1929
NW056.031

L.C.

3½

YELVERTOFT & STANFORD PARK

1899

Station originally called STANFORD HALL
Renamed YELVERTOFT 1.6.1870
Renamed YELVERTOFT & STANFORD HALL 12.1880
Renamed YELVERTOFT & STANFORD PARK 1.2.1881

DOWN MAIN
UP MAIN

5¾

5.22

L.C.

Yelvertoft S.C. 5.26
Opened 10.1878
Closed 10.7.1966
NW056.041

YELVERTOFT & STANFORD PARK STATION 5.22
Closed to Passengers 6.6.1966
Closed to Goods 6.7.1964
Siding and all connections removed 7.1965

Cold Ashby L.C.
NW056.042

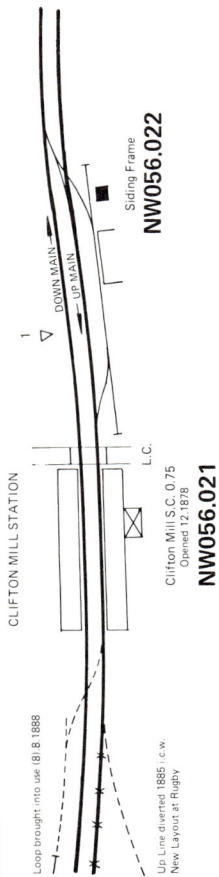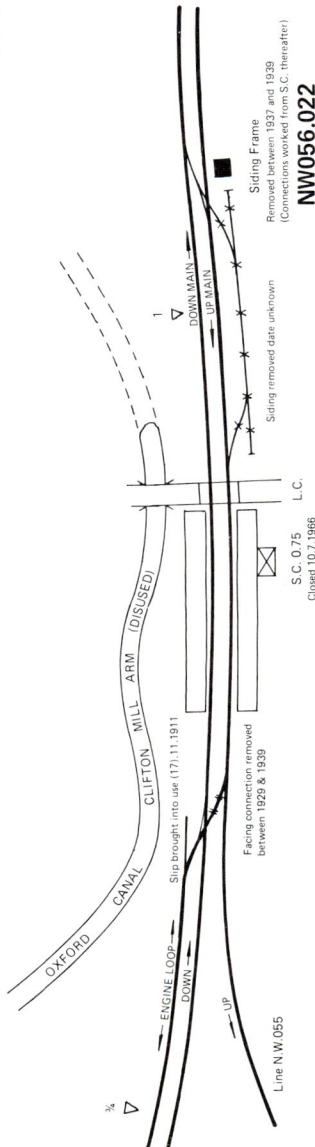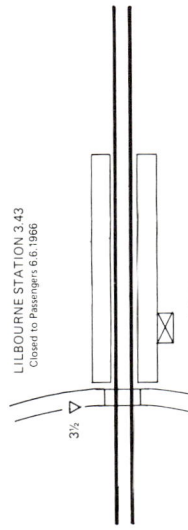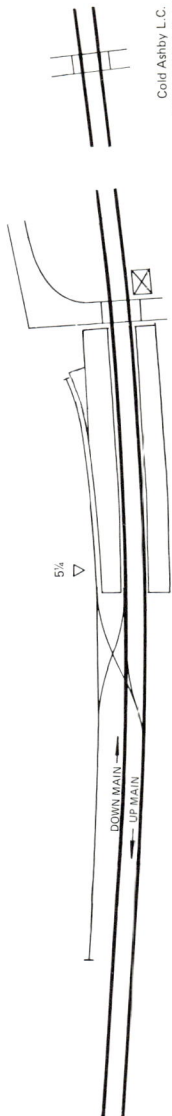

WELFORD & KILWORTH

1885

Station originally called WELFORD
Renamed WELFORD, KILWORTH b.1853
Renamed WELFORD & KILWORTH 4.1855
Renamed WELFORD & KILWORTH 11.1860?
Renamed WELFORD & KILWORTH 13.1.1913

WELFORD & KILWORTH STATION 9.20
Closed to Passengers 6.6.1966
Closed to Goods 6.7.1964
(Private Siding in use after this)

Welford S.C. 9.27
Opened 12.1878
Closed 10.7.1966

NW056.061

Alignment of former sidings to quarries
Removed by 1906

Siding removed, date unknown
(Probably post 1960)

U.R.S. 43

DOWN MAIN
UP MAIN

9½

L.C.

United Dairy Sidings
Added early 1928
Closed between 1959 and 1964

9¾

Shown as Ellis's Sidings at 1929/1960

SOUTH KILWORTH L.C.

7½

Lodge

G.F.
(? position)

South Kilworth L.C. 7.42

NW056.051

THEDDINGWORTH

1885

THEDDINGWORTH STATION 12.35
Closed to Passengers 6.6.1966
Closed to Goods 6.4.1964
Siding removed (12) 4.1964

Theddingworth S.C. 12.38
Opened 10.7.1966
Closed 10.7.1966

NW056.081

L.C.

C.P.s

DOWN MAIN
UP MAIN

HUSBANDS' BOSWORTH L.C.

G.F.

Lodge

11

Husbands' Bosworth L.C. 11.02

NW056.071

LUBENHAM

1885

DOWN MAIN
UP MAIN

LUBENHAM STATION 14.63
Closed to Passengers 6.6.1966
Closed to Goods 6.4.1964
Siding and all connections removed (12) 4.1964

Lubenham S.C. 14.60
Opened 10.1878
Closed (12) 4.1964

NW056.101

14¾

SCOBORO L.C.

Lodge

13¾

Scoboro' L.C. 13.41

NW056.091

Line originally single. Double line opened 22.7.1878
Line closed 6.6.1966. t.o.u. 10.7.1966 and all remaining lines on this page closed

MARKET HARBOROUGH

1880

From Rugby

Line from Rugby originally single
Double line opened 22.7.1878

Siding added 1883

From Northampton
See page 23
Line N W 054
Line originally single
Double line opened 4.8.1879

17¼

18¼

Northampton Junction S.C.
NW056.111

Coal Yard S.C.
NW056.112

17½

COAL YARD

Church Yard

Connection to yard added 1876, originally
facing points Altered to slip connection 1877

C.P.s

G.S.

Engine shed proposed 1864

C.P.s

M.R. from Bedford 15.4.1857
Line opened

Midland Junction S.C.
NW056.121

S.C. (? name)
NW056.125

MARKET HARBOROUGH STATION
LNW: Closed to Passengers 27.6.1885 (see below)
Replaced by new joint station with separate MR Goods Depot

1899

No. 1 S.C. 17.40
Opened 7.1885
New S.C. between 1956 and 1958, see next page
NW056.113

MARKET HARBOROUGH STATION

No. 2 S.C. 17.57
Opened 7.1885
New S.C. on site of M.R. North S.C. opened 4.1.1931
NW056.122

No. 3 S.C. 17.73
Opened 7.1885
NW056.126

17¼

18¼

17.33 = 18.39

17.38 = 18.43

17½

Br. 35

Br. 35A

COAL YARD

C.P.s

18½

17.42

South S.C. (M.R.)
Opened c.3.1885
Closed 4.1.1931

UP BAY LINE

DOWN BAY LINE

St. Mary's
Church Yard

DOWN GOODS
UP GOODS

G.S.

G.S.

Up Sidings G.F.
Brought into use 4.1.1931

Br. 29

M.R. from Bedford

Removed by 1.1931 (?)

Connections ——✕—— removed by 1954

17¼

Engine Shed
Layout altered 1920 (——new)

T.T. 42 ft

T.T. 60 ft.

Br. 36

DOWN MAIN
UP MAIN

DOWN M.R.
UP M.R.

EXCHANGE SIDINGS

17¾

C.P.s

Br. 28G

18

17.72

New Junction opened 27.7.1924

North S.C. (M.R.)
Opened c.6.1885
Closed 4.1.1931

MARKET HARBOROUGH STATION ENLARGEMENT

Alterations commenced	4.1883
New station opened	14.9.1884 (one source gives 28.6.1885)
New connections at South S.C. completed	3.1885
Opened by M.R. (?)	7&.6.1885 (but stated as complete 14.7.1885)
Full length of permanent M.R. Down platform completed	2.1886
M.R. temporary timber down platform t.o.u.	22.2.1886
Altered junction with Northampton line opened	8.8.1886

MARKET HARBOROUGH

1960

MARKET HARBOROUGH STATION 17.48

Coal Yard G.F.
NW056.115

Goods Yard G.F.
NW056 116

Line from Rugby closed 6.6.1966
t.o.u. 10.7.1966

Goods Yard closed 20.12.1965
Up and Down Goods Lines and all sidings
connected therewith t.o.u. 24.7.1966

Line to Seaton closed 6.6.1966
but retained until 1968 (?)

Ex. M. R. Line
To Leicester

18

ENGINE SHED
closed 4.10.1965

60 ft T.T.

Goods Shed

DOWN WESTERN
UP WESTERN

EXCHANGE SIDINGS

DOWN MIDLAND
UP MIDLAND

83¾

Market Harborough No. 3 S.C.
17.73 = 83.18
NW056.126

17½

DOWN GOODS
UP GOODS

DOWN BAY

Slip t.o.u. 14.5.1961

Goods Shed

83

Cattle Pens

Market Harborough No. 2 S.C.
17.57 = 83.02
NW056.123

COAL YARD

UP BAY

17½

18½

Market Harborough No. 1 S.C. 17.31
Opened between 1956 and 1958
Closed 24.7.1966
NW056.114

Up Sidings G.F.

82¾

From Northampton
See page 23
Line N W 054

17¼

18¾

From Northampton
See page 23

Line closed 15/16.8.1981
Renamed Engineers Sidings 27.2.1984

Ex. M. R. Line
From Bedford

1968

LONG NECK

Facing points removed
12/13.6.1982

19

DOWN WESTERN
UP WESTERN

EXCHANGE SIDINGS

DOWN MIDLAND
UP MIDLAND

83¾

Market Harborough No. 3 S.C. 18.78 = 83.18
Renamed Market Harborough 10.1968
Closed 29.6.1986
NW056.126

Bridge removed (?)

NW056.124
Up Western Line G.F.
Brought into use 20.10.1968

MARKET HARBOROUGH STATION 18.54
L.N.W. Platforms closed to Passengers 6.6.1966
L.N.W. Goods Depot closed 20.12.1965

18¾

Cattle Pens

83

Market Harborough No. 2 S.C. 18.62 = 83.02
Closed 20.10.1968
NW056.123

N.B. There may have been other connections at
No. 2 S.C. still in use in early 1968. If so these
were all t.o.u. 20.10.1968.

Up Sidings G.F.

82¾

18¾

GREAT BOWDEN

1880

M.R. to Leicester

DOWN MAIN
UP MAIN

18½

18½

19

N.B. Layout partly conjectural

DOWN MAIN
UP MAIN

Great Bowden Junction S.C.
(? site)

NW056.131

Separate M.R. lines and flyover brought into use 28.6.1885
and old lines reduced to sidings

Details of post-1960 alterations to ex M.R.
lines not shown in this volume

1899

M.R. to Leicester

84½

Great Bowden Sidings S.C.
(M.R.) 84.35

DOWN MAIN
UP MAIN

Extra siding added by 1924

✱—✱ Siding shortened by 1924, removed 1960

84¼

18¾

Br. 28B

18½

83¾

M.R. LINES

84

19

DOWN MAIN
UP MAIN

19¾

NW056.141

Langton S.C. 19.19
Opened 7.1885
Closed 1904 (?)

Line closed 6.6.1966
but retained until 1968 (?)

LINE NW056
Down ex L.N.W.R. slewed into Great Bowden Sidings to to/M single line
to Leicester (similar to pre-1886 junction) for single line working
during reconstruction of bridge 28B (M.R.), Up Line becoming up and
down Seaton line on Sundays 15 & 22 September 1929.
L.N.W.R. line between Market Harborough and Seaton closed
to all traffic 6.6.1966 (but retained until 1968?)

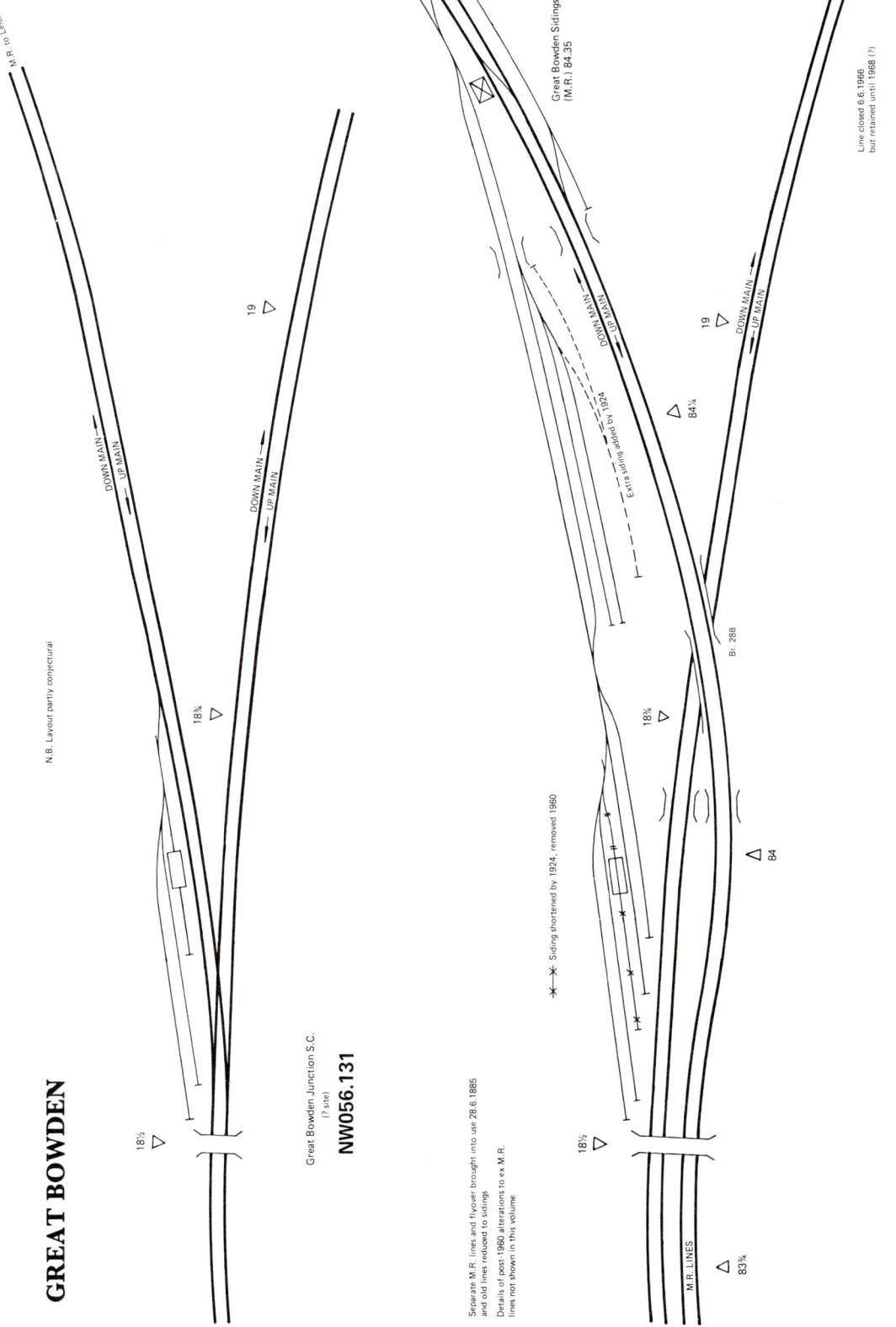

1928

Junction and G.N. & L.N.W. Joint Line opened 1.11.1879
Crossover brought into use   1881
All other lines and connections brought into use   1904
Temporary slip connection off the crossover
at Welham Junction added 1902 to allow
construction of yard

21.03 = 0.00

21

To Melton

Line N W 060
G.N. & L.N.W. Joint Line
to Melton Mowbray
(See page 35)

Welham Junction S.C. 21.03
Opened 2.1878
Closed ?

NW056.154

Removed Date unknown

1878

WELHAM BALLAST PIT

20½

Siding to quarry to allow extraction of ballast
for use in construction of the Joint Line.

Welham Ballast Pit S.C.
Opened 2.1878
Closed by 1880

NW056.152

DOWN MAIN
UP MAIN

20½

DOWN MAIN
UP MAIN

RECEPTION LINES 1
2
3

RIVER WELLAND

WELHAM SIDINGS
All sidings and connections added 1904
Yard opened 1904

Welham Sidings S.C. 20.46
Opened 1904
Reduced to G.F. between 1931 and 1933
Closed ?

NW056.153

20½

W.M.

WELHAM

Lake

20¼

Bridle Road

Lodge

Welham L.C. 20.11

NW056.151

LINE NW056
Line between Market Harborough and Seaton closed to all traffic 6.6.1966
and all remaining lines on this page closed (but retained until 1968?)

LINE NW056

WESTON L.C.

Weston L.C. 21.57
G.F. (? Position)

NW056.161

21¾ ▷

ASHLEY & WESTON　　**1885**

Station opened as MEDBOURNE BRIDGE
Renamed ASHLEY & WESTON 1.3.1878
(Official records show date as 1.1.1880)

ASHLEY & WESTON STATION 22.52
　　Closed to Passengers　18.6.1951
　　Closed to Goods　18.3.1963

NW036.171

Ashley & Weston S.C. 22.50
　　Opened　9.1879
　　Closed　8.1.1968

Goods Shed and short siding
removed, crossover added by 1928

22¾ ▷

G.F.
t.o.u. between 1916 & 1931
(points then worked from S.C.)

NW056.172

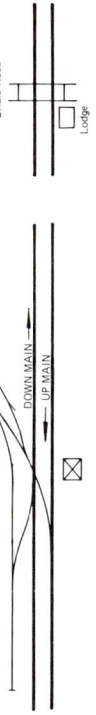

HOLTS SIDING　　**1886**

W. J. Roseby Workings opened 1861
B. Thornton 1862
Workings closed 1868, reopened 1871
Medbourne Bridge Iron Ore Co. 1871
Finally closed 1874

Holts Siding S.C.
Opened 5.1873
Closed by 1899

NW056.181

To Quarry

DOWN MAIN
UP MAIN

24 ▷

HOLT L.C.

Bridle Road

Lodge

Holt L.C. 24.01

NW056.182

DRAYTON JUNCTION

LINE NW061
G.N. & L.N.W. Joint line from Hallaton Junction
Line opened to goods 1.11.1879
(See pages 36 & 37)

Line singled (28).1.1906
Closed 1.4.1916 but retained
for wagon storage until c.1945

Temporary S.C. opened and Down line interlaced
with Up to plan dated Feb.1878 (for bridge
reconstruction)

NW056.183

Br. 44

D.R.S. 28

Drayton Junction S.C. 24.55
　　Opened　1879
　　Closed　2.1.1945

NW056.191

24.56 = 0.00

DOWN MAIN
UP MAIN

RIVER WELLAND

24¾ ▷

DRAYTON CROSSING

(Farm track)

L.C.

Lodge

Drayton Crossing　25.12

NW056.193

Drayton Wharf
Siding and G.F. brought into use (20).8.1899
Siding and G.F. removed between 1916 & 1931
Siding not private (Public goods siding?)

G.F.

NW056.192

GT. EASTON L.C.

Lodge

Bridle Road

Great Easton L.C. 26.70

NW056.201

ROCKINGHAM

Goods Shed

Cattle Pens

ROCKINGHAM STATION 27.46

Closed to Passengers　6.6.1966
Closed to goods　6.4.1964
All remaining sidings t.o.u. (26).3.1964

Crossover replaced by slip by 1929

G.F. 27.39 approx.

NW056.211

27½ ▷

DOWN MAIN
UP MAIN

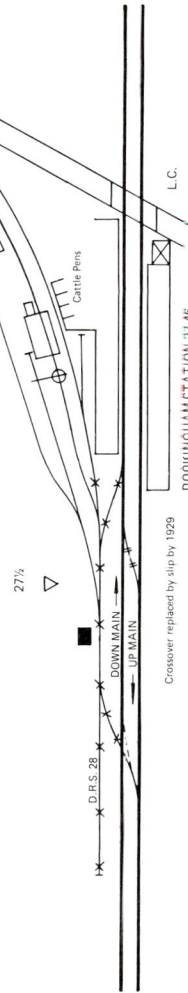

Rockingham S.C. 27.48
　　Opened　9.1879
　　Closed　28.1.1968

NW056.212

L.C.

LIDDINGTON L.C.　　**1899**

G.F.

Liddington L.C. 29.26

NW056.221

THORPE BY WATER L.C.

Lodge

G.F.

Thorpe-by-Water L.C. 30.72

NW056.222

Line between Market Harborough and Seaton closed to all traffic 6.6.1966
and all remaining lines on this page closed (but retained until 1968)

SEATON

1875

Originally SEATON & UPPINGHAM
Renamed SEATON 1.10.1894

To Luffenham

SEATON STATION

L.C.

Station Frame 31.47
Brought into use 4.1879

NW056.231

DOWN BAY

UP BAY

G.S.

L.C.

C.P.s

1885

LINE NW058
Uppingham Branch
Opened 17.9.1894

To Luffenham

Uppingham Junction S.C. 32.26
Opened 6.1894
Closed 1907

NW057.011

Junction 32.20 = 0.00

Line N.W.058
To Uppingham
(See page 34)

32¼ ▽
Br. 57

DOWN
UP

M.R. to Manton

14 △

32 ▷

Br. 56

32 △

DOWN MAIN
UP MAIN

Seaton & Wanstord Line
Opened to Goods 21.7.1879
See next page

Turntable provided Summer 1880
Replaced by Engine Shed c.1895

Seaton S.C. 31.60
Opened 4.1879

NW056.233

31¾ ▽

Junction 31.60

Site of contractor's siding
for building Wansford Line

Crossover added Sept. 1894

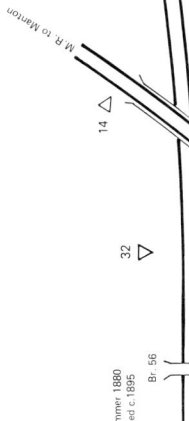

SEATON STATION 31.50

L.C.

Station Frame 31.47

NW056.231

DOWN BAY

UP BAY

C.P.s

1910

Line N.W.057

To Luffenham
(See page 34)

32¼ ▽
Br. 57

UPPINGHAM BRANCH
DOWN
UP

LUFFENHAM BRANCH
UP
DOWN

Line to Luffenham singled and Uppingham Line
Junction moved to Seaton Junction (21).7.1907

Mr from Kettering

14 △

32 ▷

Br. 56

32 △

DOWN MAIN
UP MAIN

Engine Shed

S.C. 31.60

NW056.233

31¾ ▽

Connections to Up Bay altered to
layout shown below (8).5.1949

Station Frame

NW056.232

DOWN BAY

UP BAY

C.P.s

L.C.

1960

To Luffenham

Uppingham Branch
Closed 1.6.1964

32¼ ▽
Br. 57

14 △

32 ▷

Br. 56

32 △

DOWN MAIN
UP MAIN

E.S. Closed 1961

Seaton S.C. 31.60
Closed 8.1.1968

NW056.233

31¾ ▽

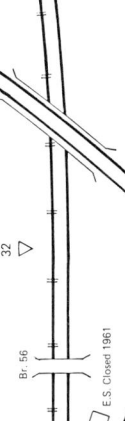

SEATON STATION 31.50
Closed to Passengers 6.6.1966
Closed to Goods 6.4.1964
Sidings removed 4.1964

Station Frame 31.47

NW056.232

DOWN BAY

UP BAY

C.P.s

L.C.

All remaining ex L.N.W.R. lines on this page closed to all traffic 6.6.1966
(Market Harborough to Luffenham Jc. retained until 1968?)

LINES NW056, NW057

31

BELL BROS. SIDING

1913

WAKERLEY & BARROWDEN

1899

DOWN MAIN
UP MAIN

Viaduct

34¼ ▽

G.F. 34.23 Approx.
NW056.241

Loader

Siding and G.F. added 1912 (by Aug.)
Pt opened 1913, closed 2.1914
P.S.A. Bell Bros. Ltd 8.7.1913
Reopened 1915 P.S.A. Marquis of Exeter 12.10.1915
Wakerley Ironstone Co. 1916
(Used by Partington Steel & Iron Co. at 6.1917)
Partington Iron & Steel Co. Ltd c.1920
Last train 1921
Sidings at G.F. removed by 1931

34¼ ▽

WAKERLEY & BARROWDEN STATION
34.65

Goods Shed

U.R.S. 36   D.R.S. 27   (Added 1937/40)

DOWN MAIN
UP MAIN

35 ▽

NW056.251

Wakerley & Barrowden
S.C. 34.76
Opened 7.1879
Closed (9).5.1965

Closed to Passengers 6.6.1966
Closed to Goods 28.12.1964
S.C. closed & all remaining connections t.o.u. (9).5.1965

MONCKTON'S SIDING

1899

Br. 12

G.F.
Brought into use 1931/3
NW056.262

DOWN MAIN
UP MAIN

36 ▽

NW056.263

Monckton's Siding S.C. 35.78
Opened 4.1881
Closed between 1931 & 1933

t.o.u.?

Br. 13

MONCKTON'S SIDING
NW056.261

P.S.A. 19.5.1873 General Whichcote & Others, E. P. Monckton
(N.B. P.S.A. date is 6 years before the line was opened)
At opening of line there was a
G.F. here replaced by S.C. 1881

LINE NW056
Line between Market Harborough and Kingscliffe closed to all traffic 6.6.1966
and all remaining lines on this page closed

KINGS CLIFFE

1900

DOWN MAIN

UP MAIN

39

Kings Cliffe S.C. 38.60
Opened 7.10.79
Closed ?

NW056.271

D.R.S. 31

38½

Deleted from Appendix between 1937 and 1940

KINGS CLIFFE STATION 38.70
Closed to Passengers 6.6.1966
Closed to Goods 3.6.1968

U.R.S. 32

Goods Shed

Line from Market Harborough closed 6.6.1966

1967

39

38½

G.F.

NW056.272

Closed to goods 3.6.1968 together with line to Naylor Benzon's Siding G.F.

NAYLOR BENZON SIDING

Naylor Benzon Mining Co. Pit opened 1939
Siding and G.F. added 1939
Nassington Barrowden Mining Co. Ltd. 3.1.1951
Naylor Benzon & Co. Ltd. 4.1956

G.F. 41.77 approx.

NW056.281

42

42½

To Quarry

Line closed 3.6.1968

Line singled 1966 (Down Line retained)

Line from Wansford retained as siding to Naylor Benzon's Quarry after 3.6.1968
Not regularly used after 4.1.1971
t.o.u.? 30.3.1971 but used for stabling Royal Train 8.9.1971
Retained until 17.2.1976 at least and traversed by Peterborough Railway
Society special train

NASSINGTON

1899

Viaduct 42.66
142 yds.

Viaduct 43.11
142 yds.

RIVER NENE

RIVER NENE

DOWN MAIN

UP MAIN

42½

42½

Nassington S.C. 42.56 approx.
Opened 7.1879
Closed (9).5.1965

NW056.291

Goods Shed

C.P.s

NASSINGTON STATION 42.47
Closed to Passengers 1.7.1957
Closed to Goods 3.8.1957
S.C. closed, and all remaining connections t.o.u. (9).5.1965
Line singled 1966 (Down line retained)

To Yarwell Junction
See page 19
Line N.W.051

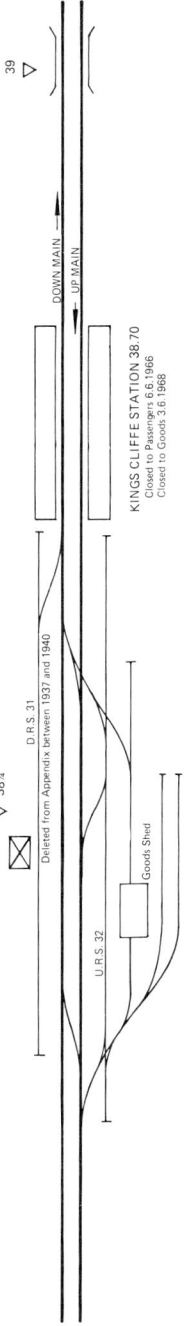
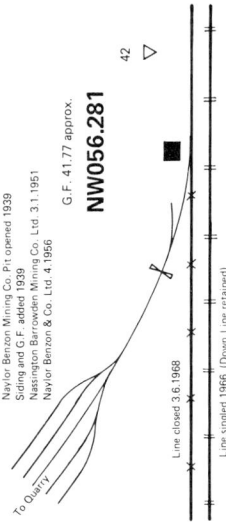
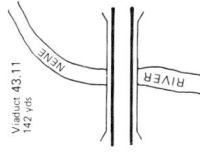
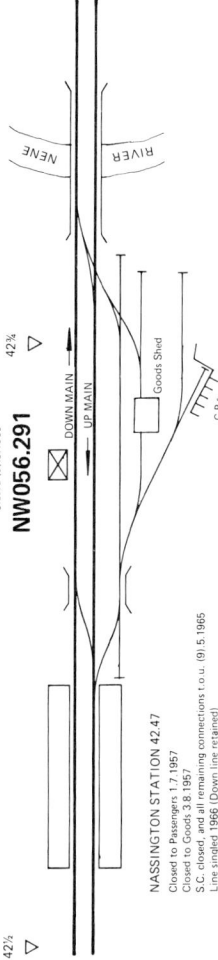

MORCOTT

NW057.021

Platform Frame
Brought into use 10.1898
t.o.u. 2.1901

NW057.022

Morcott S.C. 33.68
Opened 2.1901
Closed 7.1907

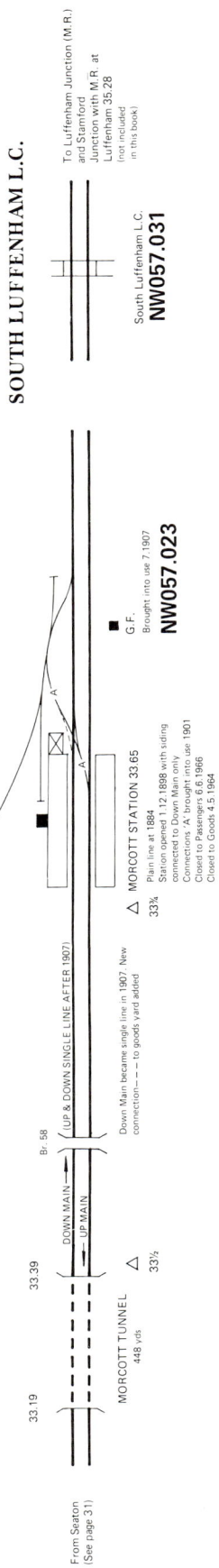

1902

SOUTH LUFFENHAM L.C.

To Luffenham Junction (M.R.)
and Stamford
Junction with M.R. at
Luffenham 35.28
(not included
in this book)

South Luffenham L.C.
NW057.031

G.F.
Brought into use 7.1907
NW057.023

33.19   33.39   Br. 58

(UP & DOWN SINGLE LINE AFTER 1907)

From Seaton
(See page 31)

DOWN MAIN
UP MAIN

MORCOTT TUNNEL
448 yds

33½

Down Main became single line in 1907. New
connection -- - to goods yard added

MORCOTT STATION 33.65

Plain line at 1884
Station opened 1.12.1898 with siding
connected to Down Main only
Connections 'A' brought into use 1901
Closed to Passengers 6.6.1966
Closed to Goods 4.5.1964

33¾

LINE N.W.057 SEATON JUNCTION TO LUFFENHAM JUNCTION (MIDLAND)
Line singled 21.7.1907 (former Down line retained as single line)
Line closed to all traffic 6.6.1966 and all remaining lines on this page closed (but
retained until 1968?)

UPPINGHAM

1902

UPPINGHAM STATION 3.12
Closed to Passengers 13.6.1960
Closed to Goods 1.6.1964

Ilnningham Station Frame 3.13
Brought into use 6.1894
NW057.022

3.15

Goods Shed

NW058.021

3   G.F. 3.01

To Quarries

Quarry Siding installed (19).10.1912
P.S.A. 14.10.1912 J. Pain Ltd.
Siding removed between 1916 and 1929

2%

2.61

Viaduct No. 6 74 yds approx.

G F (?min'mn)
2.54 approx.
NW058.011

Br. 5

From Seaton
(See page 31)

LINE N.W.058 UPPINGHAM BRANCH
Opened to Goods 17.9.1894
Opened to Passengers 1.10.1894
Closed to Passengers 13.6.1960
Closed to Goods 1.6.1964

It is believed that the layout shown below was
brought into use from the date of the line opening

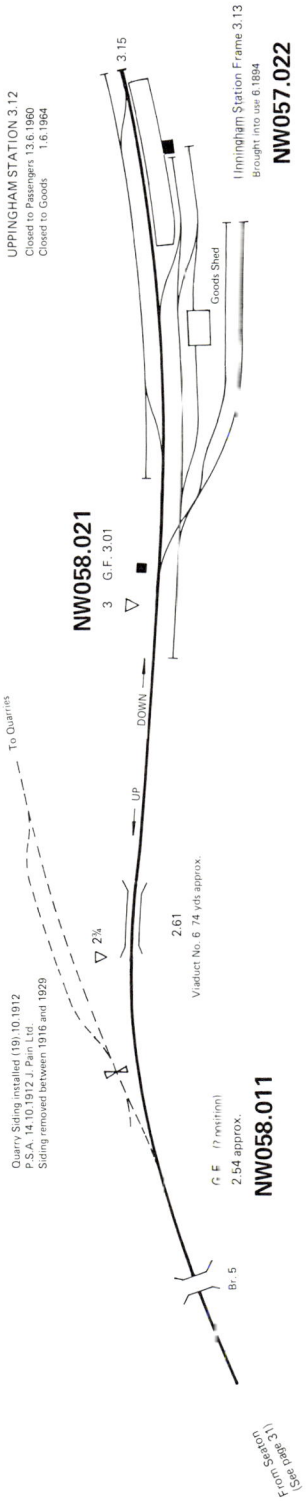

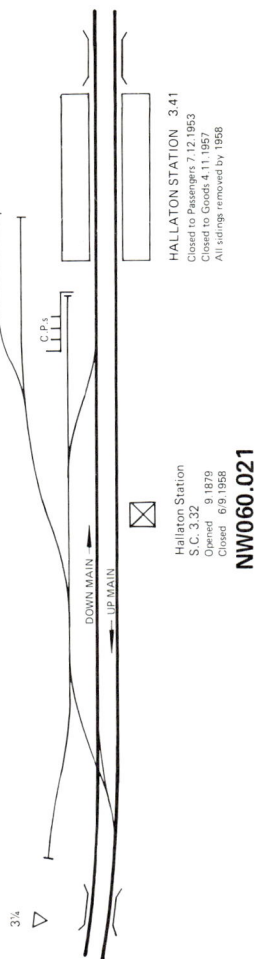

LINE N.W.060 G.N. & L.N.W. JOINT WELHAM JUNCTION TO MELTON MOWBRAY
Line opened to Goods
From Bottesford to Melton Mowbray 30.6.1879
To Twyford 13.10.1879
To Welham Junction 1.11.1879
Line opened to Passengers
From Bottesford to Melton Mowbray 1.9.1879
To Welham 15.12.1879
All stations closed to Passengers 7.12.1953 (except John O'Gaunt & East Norton)
Line closed Welham Junction to Marefield Junction North 4.11.1963
and all remaining lines on this page closed
Leicester...
Melton Mowbray to Stathern Ironstone Sidings closed 7.9.1964

Through local passenger services withdrawn 7.12.1953
Passenger service between Leicester and John O'Gaunt retained until 29.4.1957
Unadvertised service of workmen's trains between Market Harborough and
East Norton only, retained until 20.5.1957

1885

HALLATON

3½

C.P.s

DOWN MAIN
UP MAIN

HALLATON STATION 3.41
Closed to Passengers 7.12.1953
Closed to Goods 4.11.1957
All sidings removed by 1958

Hallaton Station
S.C. 3.32
Opened 9.1879
Closed 6.9.1958

NW060.021

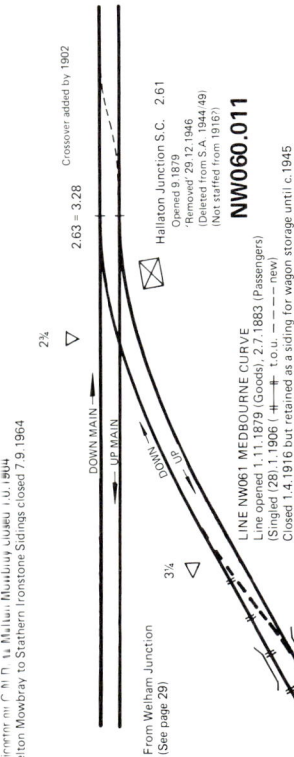

1885

HALLATON JUNCTION

3¾

2¾

2.63 = 3.28   Crossover added by 1902

DOWN MAIN
UP MAIN
DOWN
UP

Hallaton Junction S.C. 2.61
Opened 9.1879
'Removed 29.12.1946
(Deleted from S.A. 1944/49)
(Not staffed from 1916?)

NW060.011

LINE NW061 MEDBOURNE CURVE
Line opened 1.11.1879 (Goods), 2.7.1883 (Passengers)
(Singled (28).1.1906 (+──────+ t.o.u. ─ ─ ─ new)
Closed 1.4.1916 but retained as a siding for wagon storage until c.1945

From Welham Junction
(See page 29)

From Drayton Junction
(See pages 37 & 30)
Line N.W.061

5.19   5.37

East Norton
Tunnel 444 yds

EAST NORTON

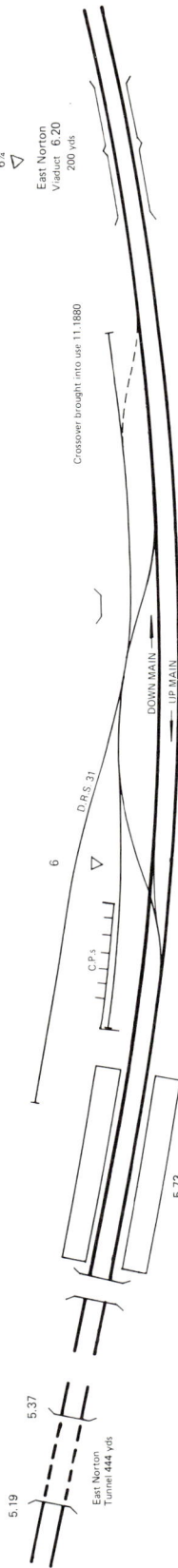

1885

6¾

East Norton
Viaduct 6.20
200 yds

Crossover brought into use 11.1880

D.R.S. 31

6

DOWN MAIN
UP MAIN

C.P.s

East Norton S.C. 6.02
Opened 9.1879
Closed ?

NW060.031

5.73

EAST NORTON STATION
Closed to Passengers 7.12.1953
Except workmen's train which
continued until 20.5.1957
Closed to Goods 4.11.1963

1902

TILTON

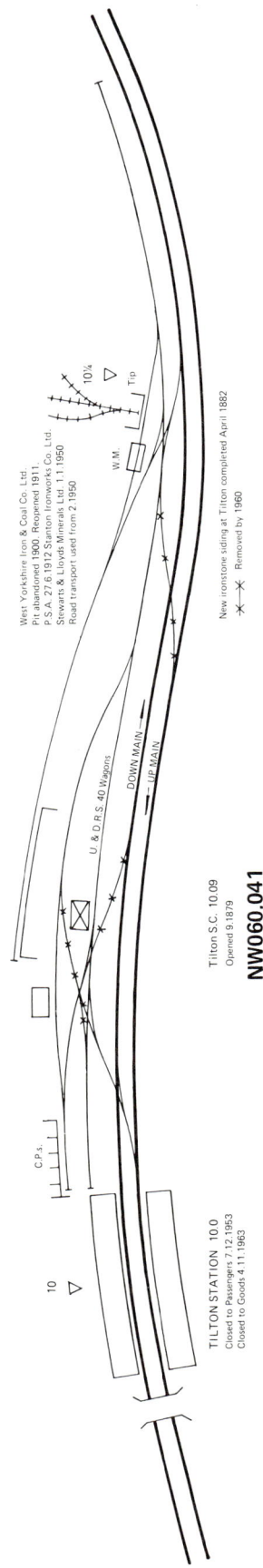

West Yorkshire Iron & Coal Co. Ltd.
Pit abandoned 1900. Reopened 1911.
P.S.A. 27.6.1912 Stanton Ironworks Co.Ltd.
Stewarts & Lloyds Minerals Ltd. 1.1.1950
Road transport used from 2.1950

New ironstone siding at Tilton completed April 1882

──×── Removed by 1960

10¾
Tip
W.M.

U. & D.R.S. 40 Wagons

DOWN MAIN
UP MAIN

C.P.s

10

TILTON STATION 10.0
Closed to Passengers 7.12.1953
Closed to Goods 4.11.1963

Tilton S.C. 10.09
Opened 9.1879

NW060.041

LINE NW060   35

MAREFIELD JUNCTION SOUTH

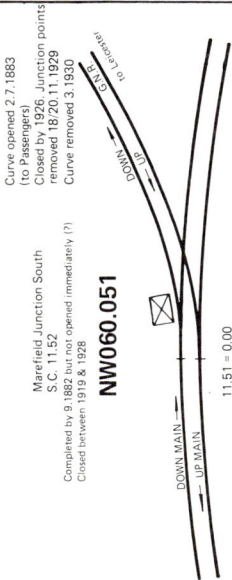

Marefield Junction South
S.C. 11.52
Completed by 9.1882 but not opened immediately (?)
Closed between 1919 & 1928

NW060.051

11.51 = 0.00

Curve opened 2.7.1883
(to Passengers)
Closed by 1926. Junction points
removed 18/20.11.1929
Curve removed 3.1930

DOWN MAIN
UP MAIN
G.N.R. to Leicester

JOHN O'GAUNT

Station originally called BURROW & TWYFORD
Renamed JOHN O'GAUNT 25.6.1883 (according to L.N.W. records)
(2.7.1883 according to G.N. Records)

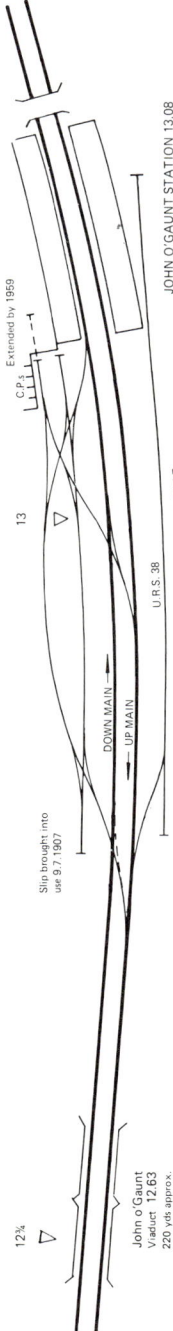

12¾

John o'Gaunt
Viaduct 12.63
220 yds approx.

MAREFIELD JUNCTION NORTH   **1883**

Line south of Marefield Junction North closed 4.11.1963 (+—+)
Line to Leicester closed 1.6.1964
(On opening of new link from ex M.R. line)

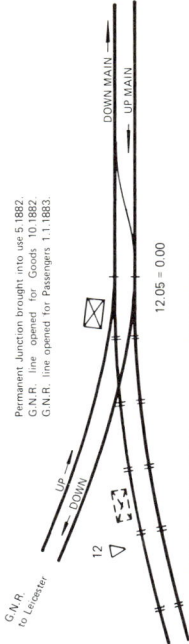

DOWN MAIN
UP MAIN

12.05 = 0.00

Permanent Junction brought into use 5.1882.
G.N.R. line opened for Goods 10.1882.
G.N.R. line opened for Passengers 1.1.1883.

Marefield Junction North
S.C. 12.04
Opened 1880
Closed 1911

NW060.052   **1902**

Marefield Junction North
S.C. 12.01
Opened 1911
Closed 1963 (?)

NW060.053

UP
DOWN
G.N.R. to Leicester
12
S.C.

Marefield Junction North

Temporary arrangement brought
into use 8.1880 for Contractor's Siding

Extended by 1959
C.P.s
13
U.R.S. 38
DOWN MAIN
UP MAIN

Slip brought into
use 9.7.1907

JOHN O'GAUNT STATION 13.08
(Terminus of service from Leicester
after 7.12.1953)
Closed to Passengers 29.4.1957
Closed to Goods 4.11.1963

John O'Gaunt S.C. 12.79
Opened 9.1879
New Cabin opened 10.1911 at 13.00
replacing old Cabin.
New Cabin closed ?

**NW060.061
NW060.062**   **1902**

GREAT DALBY

Great Dalby   S.C. 16.38
Opened 9.1879
Closed 9.1953/6.1954

NW060.071

16½
D.R.S. 37

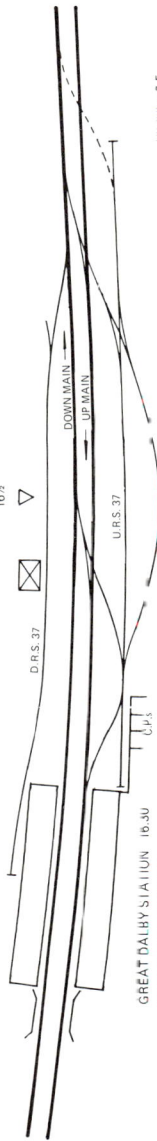

GREAT DALBY STATION 16.30
Closed to Passengers 7.12.1953
Closed to Goods 7.12.1953
All sidings removed by 1954

DOWN MAIN
UP MAIN
U.R.S. 37
C.P.s

Up siding G.r.
added 1943/4

NW060.072

Line from Welham Junction to Marefield Junction North closed 4.11.1963
Line from Marefield Junction North to Melton Mowbray closed 1.6.1964
and all remaining lines on this page closed

SYSONBY JUNCTION

1883

Sysonby Junction S.C.
Opened 1879
Closed 18.4.1887

NW060.081

DOWN MAIN
UP MAIN

LINE NW.062

TO M.F.R.

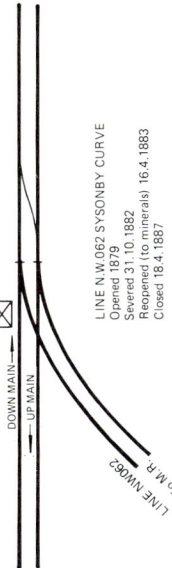

LINE N.W.062 SYSONBY CURVE
Opened 1879
Severed 31.10.1882
Reopened (to minerals) 16.4.1883
Closed 18.4.1887

MELTON MOWBRAY

Goods Station only renamed MELTON MOWBRAY NORTH 1.7.1950

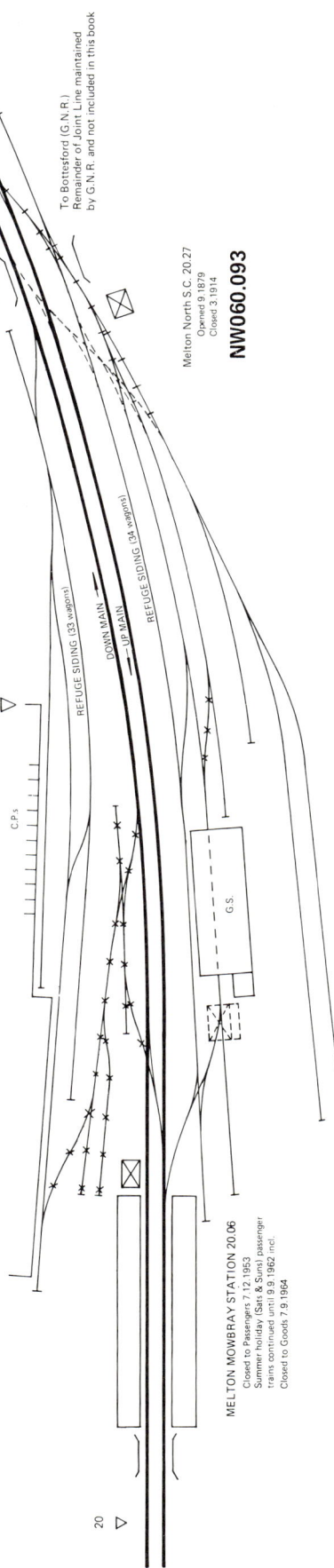

1902

1902

Connections altered (1).3.1914
in connection with new S.C.
+ — removed — — new

To Bottesford (G.N.R.)
Remainder of Joint Line maintained
by G.N.R. and not included in this book

Br. 81

Melton North S.C. 20.27
Opened 9.1879
Closed 3.1914

NW060.093

LINE NW060
Line from Marefield Junction North to Melton Mowbray closed 1.6.1964
Line from Melton Mowbray to Stathern Ironstone Sidings closed 7.9.1964
and all remaining lines on this page closed.

REFUGE SIDING (33 wagons)
DOWN MAIN
UP MAIN
REFUGE SIDING (34 wagons)

C.P.s

G.S.

20½

Melton Mowbray S.C. 20.14
Opened 3.1914
Closed ?

NW060.092

MELTON MOWBRAY STATION 20.06
Closed to Passengers 7.12.1953
Summer holiday (Sats. & Suns) passenger
trains continued until 9.9.1962 incl.
Closed to Goods 7.9.1964

Melton South S.C. 20.10
Opened 9.1879
Closed 3.1914

NW060.091

Line closed south of Melton Mowbray
(to Leicester) 1.6.1964

20

MEDBOURNE

1885

1885

To Hallaton Junction
(see Page 35)

DOWN MAIN
UP MAIN

C.P.s

NW061.011
NW061.012
NW061.013

Medbourne S.C. 2.11
Opened 9.1879
Closed 1.1906
(Two G.F.s brought into use
sites unknown)

MEDBOURNE STATION 2.07
Closed to Passengers 1.4.1916
Closed to Goods 1.4.1916

From Drayton Junction
(see page 30)

2

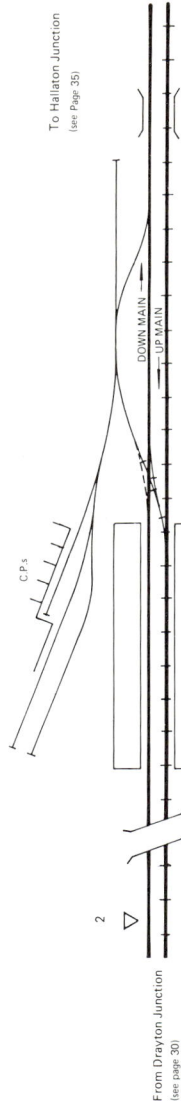

LINE N.W.061 MEDBOURNE CURVE
Opened to Goods 1.11.1879
Opened to Passengers 2.7.1883
Singled (28).1.1906
Closed to traffic 1.4.1916 but retained as siding
for wagon storage until c.1945

Line singled (28).1.1906 (++t.o.u. — new)
Closed to traffic 1.4.1916

LINES NW060, NW061, NW062

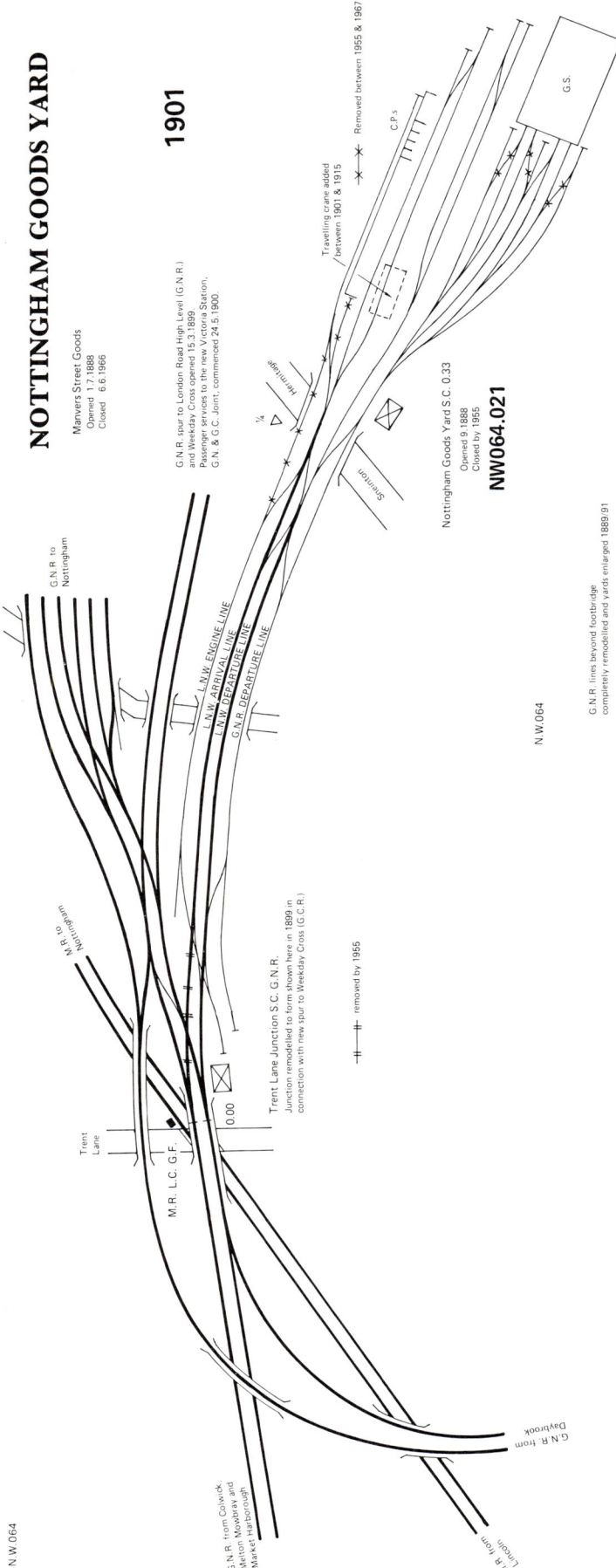
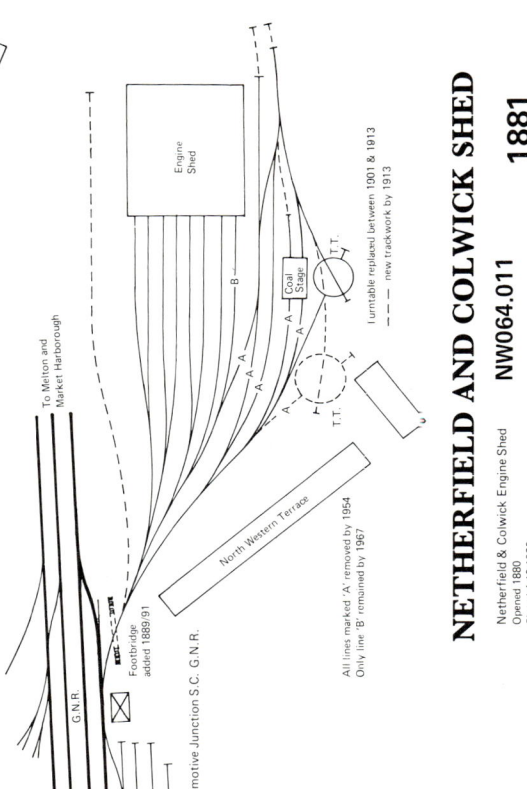
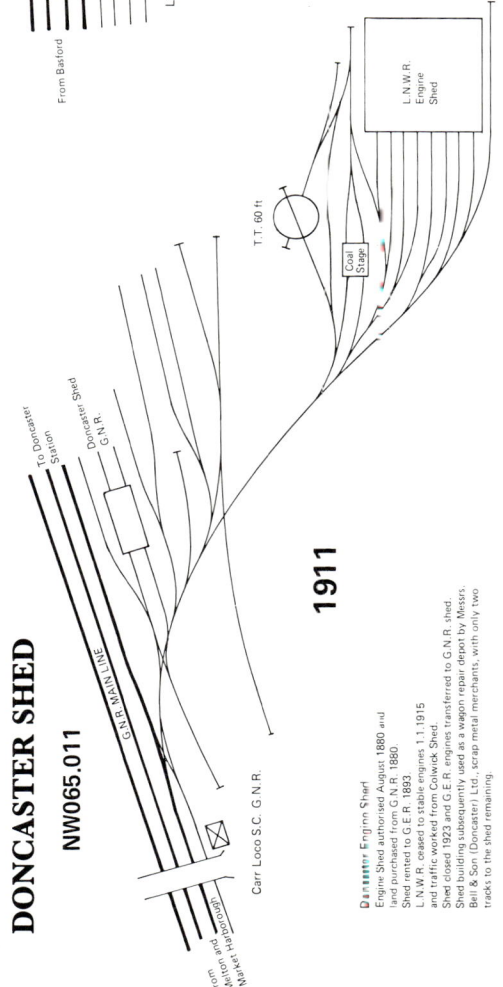

NOTTINGHAM GOODS YARD

1901

Manvers Street Goods
Opened 1.7.1888
Closed 6.6.1966

G.N.R. spur to London Road High Level (G.N.R.)
and Weekday Cross opened 15.3.1899.
Passenger services to the new Victoria Station,
G.N. & G.C. Joint, commenced 24.5.1900.

Nottingham Goods Yard S.C. 0.33

Opened 9.1888
Closed by 1955

NW064.021

Removed between 1955 & 1967

C.P.s

Travelling crane added
between 1901 & 1915

G.S.

N.W.064

Trent Lane Junction S.C. G.N.R.
Junction remodelled to form shown here in 1889 in
connection with new spur to Weekday Cross (G.C.R.)

— removed by 1955

G.N.R. to
Nottingham

M.R. to
Nottingham

L.N.W. ENGINE LINE
L.N.W. ARRIVAL LINE
L.N.W. DEPARTURE LINE
G.N.R. DEPARTURE LINE

Trent Lane
M.R. L.C. G.F.

0.00

G.N.R. from
Daybrook

G.N.R. from Colwick,
Melton Mowbray and
Market Harborough

M.R. from
Lincoln

NETHERFIELD AND COLWICK SHED

1881

NW064.011

Netherfield & Colwick Engine Shed
Opened 1880
Closed 4.12.1932
Shed subsequently used as a wagon works

Engine Shed

To Melton and
Market Harborough

turntable replaced between 1901 & 1913
--- new trackwork by 1913

Coal Stage
T.T.
A A
A A
A

All lines marked 'A' removed by 1954
Only line 'B' remained by 1967

North Western Terrace

Footbridge
added 1889/91

Locomotive Junction S.C. G.N.R.

From Basford

G.N.R. lines beyond footbridge
completely remodelled and yards enlarged 1889/91

G.N.R.

DONCASTER SHED

1911

NW065.011

N.W.065

Doncaster Engine Shed

Engine Shed authorised August 1880 and
land purchased from G.N.R 1880.
Shed rented to G.E.R 1893
L.N.W.R. ceased to stable engines 1.1.1915
and traffic worked from Colwick Shed.
Shed closed 1923 and G.E.R. engines transferred to G.N.R. shed.
Shed building subsequently used as a wagon repair depot by Messrs.
Bell & Son (Doncaster) Ltd, scrap metal merchants, with only two
tracks to the shed remaining.

L.N.W.R
Engine
Shed

Coal Stage
T.T. 60 ft

To Doncaster
Station

Doncaster Shed
G.N.R.

Carr Loco S.C. G.N.R.

From and
Melton and
Market Harborough

G.N.R. MAIN LINE

N.W.064

LINE ORDER LIST OF LOCATIONS

ALPHABETIC LIST OF LOCATIONS